Get Clients 101 – The Essential Handbook for Coaches and Consultants

Jo Dale

Get Clients 101 - The Essential Handbook for Coaches
and Consultants

by Jo Dale

Crescendo Publishing, LLC
300 Carlsbad Village Drive
Ste. 108A, #443
Carlsbad, California 92008-2999

Cover Design by Melodye Hunter

ISBN: 978-0-9909974-0-5 (p)
ISBN: 978-0-9909974-1-2 (e:)

A Message from the Author...

Go to the link below to hear a personal message from Jo Dale, Author of *Get Clients 101: The Essential Handbook for Coaches and Consultants*

http://bit.ly/MessageFromJo

CONTENTS

INTRODUCTION

If you've picked up this book, then chances are you're a coach or consultant. Maybe you recently started out, or maybe you're established and curious as to what you could be doing differently to get clients and grow your business.

Or maybe you're wondering if setting up a coaching/consultancy business is for you.

Whoever you are, I hope that this book truly acts as a handbook for you. A book you can dip in and out of, a book that will provide you with answers and exercises and different perspectives to help you grow your business.

I will walk you through the stages from setup (where the stuff you think will be difficult is often easy and vice versa) to upscaling. This is about taking each step with *you* at the centre, creating a thriving, exciting business.

Throughout, I will give you a combination of ideas, tips, exercises, suggestions, and the occasional piece of straight talking.

I want you to be successful, and you need to believe

that you will be successful (which is why there is a whole chapter of mindset exercises). This will help you dig in on the hard days and be proud to shout from the treetops when it's time to celebrate.

If you're a coach, then I want you to think about how you can also be a consultant, and if you're a consultant, you want to add coaching to your toolkit. I will talk more about this and share with you how to position yourself, whether that's through your niche or your expertise right up front.

This book is about getting your business flying and making it sustainable. I'm very keen to help you reduce the amount of time you spend selling and increase the time you spend focusing on how to get repeat and referral business. By making the most of your expertise and serving your clients brilliantly, you will generate profit with elegance and integrity.

I set up my own coaching/consulting business over ten years ago when one day I walked into my corporate job and resigned. I had nowhere to go; I just knew I needed to do something different. Coming from a family who had always been self-employed, I had spent my youth adamant that I wouldn't take the same path, and yet I realised it was the only way I was going to spend more time doing what I love, working with people I wanted to be with, and having the freedom I craved. I only wish I had found a guide of some sort to help me think about the real fundamentals of setting up a service-based business all that time ago

I zigzagged about—a lot! And on reflection, I could have made growing my business a whole heap easier.

That's much of what I want to share with you here.

However, I have met some wonderful people and had the chance to create some real transformation for others, and it's been incredibly enjoyable and fulfilling.

So I want to share with you some of the critical ways and means for you to grow your own business so that you too are doing what you love and feeling a real sense of purpose and fulfilment.

I will share with you how to get crystal clear on the transformation you are offering your clients, how to design that transformation in a way clients love and that keeps them coming back for more, and all the other steps you can take to create a six-figure business and beyond.

Remember—create, captivate, and connect. Do these three things and you'll achieve your dream.

Are you ready?

Let's get going.

.

Foundations

*'If you have built castles in the air, your work need not be lost;
that is where they should be. Now put the foundations under them.'*

– Henry David Thoreau

If you've picked this book up, you're likely thinking of working for yourself or you already are.

It's important to know why you want to work for yourself as it will inform how you structure your business. That structure could be about where you work, with whom you work, or how much of your time you want to spend working. The joy of working for yourself is you get to be the decision maker on all three things— you just need to make good decisions so that both you and your business are healthy and happy.

People often start a new business because they're looking for flexibility, freedom, and/or a chance to be in charge of their own destinies, and yet so many forget that to have all of that they must set some boundaries to achieve it. Time is one of those boundaries you want to set first. Let's look at why.

Time

When you run your own business, it's easy to get distracted. If you're anything like me—a bit of an explorer—anything new, shiny, and bright that comes along creates a distraction. Before you know it, you're at the end of the week, and when you look back, you see very little progress for what feels like a lot of effort. (Can you imagine the discipline I needed to put pen to paper for this book!)

Deciding how much time you want to work enables you to set some parameters (otherwise known as discipline!). Once you've set these parameters, you can look at how you're planning to use this time and work out whether it brings you the revenue you dream of!

There are some simple maths to do here. To make it easy, you can go to www.getclients101.com/toolkit to download the time calculator. Play around with it to see what your working life might look like going forward.

When you're thinking about how many hours or days per week you want to work, start off with your perfect world first—dream a little. It is far better to stretch that band and let it ping back a bit than to start off small.

So in your perfect world, how many days would you like to work each week? By *work*, I mean carry out work-related tasks, whether that's at your desk or with a client.

Do you want to work five days? Fewer than five days? What would feel good for you?

My scheduled plan is to work four days a week, which means I get to have at least the equivalent of one day a week to do totally non-work things. That might be going to yoga, going to the beach, or just pootling around the house. That's a whole day a week when I do whatever I like. You may choose to work more or less. You may have dependents with whom you may want to spend more free time. You may want to work just three days a week and have two days of total freedom. You might be very happy working five days. Do what is right for you.

Remember, right now we're just going to figure out how many days you are going to work. Ultimately, we need to do this across a twelve-month period so that you can move to the next step and work out how much you will earn.

To give you an example, let's imagine you want to work four days per week. And to get started, let's agree that there are fifty-two weeks in a year.

But, of course, you want holiday, so you need to plan for that. You may want to make an allowance for dependents. (This may mean you work five short days instead of four long ones, but the hours are the same.) Are there other commitments?

Let's start to work it through:

We said there are fifty-two weeks in the year, but you're not likely going to work every single week. Plus, you must plan for holidays, etc., so let's take six weeks out for holidays, commitments, and so on. If you want to take more, just adjust the figure accordingly. It's important to be realistic about this up front. If you're not, when you get to the end of the year, you will be scratching your head wondering why you didn't meet your money goals!

Many coaches and consultants find that it gets really quiet over the key holiday periods like Christmas or Easter, so to keep things real, let's take another three weeks out for when our clients don't want to work with us.

This already means we've identified nine weeks of the year when you probably won't be working, which means you have forty-three weeks left to play with.

Great, so we have forty-three weeks when, for the sake of this example, you will be working four days each week. Let's multiply those two numbers (43 x 4), which gives us 172 days across the year. Knowing this number will help you get realistic about what the year looks like, and it will help you plan how and when you want to work.

To help you keep on track, I suggest you divide this figure by twelve (172 / 12) so that you get a monthly average of days to work. The average comes out at just over fourteen days per month. Remember, though, this is an average and takes into account the months when you might be available for work for only two weeks because of holidays, or December when you might work for only a week.

The key thing to remember is that the number of days you work each month will go up and down. You need to hold onto the long view that your *average* is around fourteen. This helps reduce panic during the quiet months and helps you keep an eye on when you need to give your business a boost!

You may look at this and say, 'That's not exactly rocket science', but you would be amazed how many people don't think about this. Instead, they wonder why running their own business becomes so exhausting.

So great! You've established how much you want to work. Remember, this encompasses all your work, whether that is time you can bill to clients or whether that's time spent doing your monthly invoicing—time you can't bill to anyone but yourself.

Days per week: 4

Weeks per year: 52 − 9 = 43

Days available for work: 43 x 4 = 172

Average workdays per month: 14.3333 (but let's say 14 to make it easier)

Remember, you can come back and do these calculations time and again with different numbers to see how it looks. I know you'll want to once you start working on the next two steps—looking at how much you want to earn and what it is you really want to do.

This is when the magic starts. Your business will move from dream to reality, and I'm here to give you the steps to make sure that happens!

So let's talk money!

Money

Money is such a prickly topic. I know from experience that it's not just the British who are reserved in sharing their thoughts, opinions, and feelings about money.

However, no matter how icky or nervous or excited or motivated you feel about money, it is money that moves what you do from a hobby to a business. You need to get comfortable with money. Your attitude toward it and learning how to make the most of it are all essential to your success.

I want you to avoid coming up with a figure that is 'enough'—you know, that amount that will pay the bills, give you a bit of pocket money, and that means you tick along fine. Approaching this from that point of view will prevent you from seizing opportunity and developing your potential, which in turn means you deprive your clients of both opportunity and potential too—something I know you don't want.

So let's take a few moments to really dream about what you want to earn.

I want you to start by thinking big. Equally important, I want you to find your motivation as to why you want to earn that amount.

Only after you've done this will we look at how what you want to earn connects with how much time you want to spend working. Pragmatists, hang in there.

What would you do if you had more money?

Get a pen and paper and make a list. Let the ideas flow. And here's the thing: at the beginning, some obvious items come to mind—paying off credit card bills, clearing the mortgage, taking nicer holidays, etc.

Then you might move to things like travelling first class, helping friends and family ease their own financial burdens, buying that Sunseeker cruiser or second holiday home. We're all different, so what will it be for you?

And after those items, what then? What if you now have all of those things?

The bills have been cleared, the friends and family have been helped, and the lifestyle purchases have been made.

What would you do next?

As you start to tap into far deeper motivations and desires that you have for your life, this is when it gets really interesting.

What else would you do? Invest in yourself and/or your business? Do more for your favourite charity? Create more time to help out in your local community? Set up a fund for young people? Provide support to those less able? Become a trustee on a board?

Keep building your list. Earning money for the sake of it is of little importance to most of us. Few are truly happy because of the amount they have in their bank account. Happiness will come from what you do with it.

I have all sorts of ideas of what I would do with more money. Outside work, I'm currently able to do a whole host of unpaid activities. I'm a pro bono business mentor for start-up businesses in my county, I run a businesswomen's network locally, and I've given time to a job club helping those out of work get back into it. None of this would be possible if I wasn't earning good money.

If you don't understand what you would do with money, it's really easy to stay small and earn enough just to pay the bills and get by. It's an attitude that hurts your business because it's not great role-modelling for your clients, and—more importantly—investing in you means your clients get even more!

Many of us are not driven by hefty egos and the need to be seen as successful (sure, some are), but it is important to have a goal and know what you would do with the money that you earn. Having these goals prevents money from creating feelings of excess and exacerbating any unworthiness that might be lurking in your mind.

Money creates freedom of choice for you and those close to you, so with that lecture over, let's get down to what this means.

Look at the list you made, and ask yourself the question: 'How much do I want to earn?'

Write that number down. Don't panic. If it's a huge number, I'm not suggesting you will pull it off in your first twelve months, but the great thing is that you now have a target, something to plan towards and something that creates another parameter (much like setting how much time you want to work) to add into the mix.

We're now going to do another bit of simple maths. I'm going to pick a conservative number out of the hat to get us started with an example.

Let's say in the next twelve months you want to earn 60,000 (put the currency symbol that works for you in front of this). This is a conservative figure for anyone coaching/consulting, by the way. You'll see why in a minute. (Ten years ago when I started up, I created 50,000 in revenue in my first year, and that was with no help or guidance!)

Before we bring in the calculations you did in the previous chapter, let's establish your average monthly income target—60,000 divided by twelve. Your monthly target is 5,000.

So, you're in good shape. You know that you want to work an average of fourteen days a month, and you know you want to earn 5,000 each month.

You are probably reaching for the calculator right now to start working out a day rate. Try not to do that. Why? First, you're not likely to do chargeable work every day you work. Second, working from a day-rate mindset can be restraining when it comes to looking at what you do and how you do it.

[Side note: Day rates do form a big part of how consultants charge for work, and organisations are used to talking in day-rate language.] Consequently, you need to have an answer ready, but wherever possible you want to package and programme what you do—particularly when it comes to coaching work—as it benefits both you and your clients. More on this in the Creating

Revenue Streams section.

Instead of worrying about the day rate right now, just note down your average number of days to work and your average earnings per month and know that it will all become clear as we start to explore what exactly it is you're going to do and how you will do it!

You will then be ready to design your business in a way that creates choice and freedom.

To love your business, you need to do something you love. Let's find out exactly what that is.

Finding your sweet spot

You don't have to be a golfer to understand what a sweet spot is. It's that perfect place where everything works. For a golfer, it's about hitting the ball using the exact right spot on the club so that the ball soars into the air and goes exactly where you want it.

For you, finding your sweet spot is essential to making work feel easy, to creating energy (not exhaustion), and to waking up every day wanting to do what it is you do.

Therefore, this chapter is all about helping you understand how to work in a way that makes your heart soar (like that golf ball). When you know where your sweet spot is, I promise you your confidence will rocket.

Right now, I have one favour to ask of you: Work through this with curiosity. Be ready to find out things about yourself that you maybe didn't know, or things that you're choosing to ignore because they don't fit with your current plans.

I am operating throughout this book under the assumption that you want to create a lasting business. If that's true, then, quite simply, you want to do what you love in a way that you love!

Let's talk about what you're really good at. Let's discover where your true strengths lie and what that means for your business. This is exciting because when you create clarity on this, a whole ton of tasks become easy—everything from writing marketing copy and proposals to designing and delivering programmes. It even makes networking a doddle!

When we work in a place of true strength, we tend to find it easy. It makes us feel energised, alive, and … well, basically happy!

Sure, there will always be tasks that have to be done that you don't like to do or that feel like they suck the life out of you. That's part of running your business. But as your business grows, you can let go of what you're not good at and spend more of your time doing what you are good at. This means it's super important that the core of what you do, that what you offer and the services you provide all use your strengths. You need to be using the expertise and skills that make you want to get out of bed in the morning, that make you light up when that e-mail comes in from a perfect potential client, and that let you go to sleep satisfied with what you have achieved.

But before we get into how you determine your core strengths, let me share a personal revelation with you.

I'm a naturally curious person. I also love learning new things and passing those lessons on. Give me a huge mess, and I rub my hands together with glee that I get the chance to get it sorted out. I love making something easy that others assume is difficult. I love working with people and getting to know them so that they can create transformation.

I'm not a fan of being in the limelight. I'm not good at doing repetitive tasks. I like working with people once I get to know them a bit—a room full of strangers makes me a little nervous.

From the first paragraph you can easily see why I'm

in the field of leadership development. You can probably also see why I'm a coach and a consultant. Working with organisations and individuals gives me a great opportunity to do all of those things I love doing.

However, as I don't crave being in the limelight, standing up in front of a bunch of people I've never met doesn't make my heart sing. So why do I MC conferences and run multiple workshops for organisations? (And, by the way, I do so really well!) It's because in doing so, I get to see people grow. I love watching the relief on someone's face when they realise it's not going to be as tough as they thought. I love transformation, big and small. And it's because all of these things matter to me that I'm prepared to do things that don't come naturally.

I use my strengths to compensate for what isn't a natural strength.

The weird thing is I keep getting asked to do this type of activity because people think I'm good at it. What has happened is I've learned to be good at it. But because it's learned behaviour, it takes up more energy, so I'm careful to balance how much of this type of work I do versus the coaching, diagnostics, facilitation, etc. that actually give me my energy back. So when it comes to unearthing your own strengths, there are two things you need to be really careful of.

Firstly, you are probably really good at doing some tasks that others find difficult, but you may not even know it. The next time someone says to you, 'You are SO good at doing that!' and you simply shrug your shoulders or raise your eyebrows with a throwaway comment of 'It's nothing', there's a good chance that whatever it was you were doing is something you find so easy you don't think twice about it. That's a real strength.

Secondly, don't believe that everything you are really good at is a real strength. Remember my learned strength of presenting and working with large crowds? Your learned strengths are ones you are really good at, but at the end of the day, you feel wrung out and exhausted, and you know you wouldn't want to repeat that day all over again anytime soon.

The exercise for you in this chapter is simple. Look back over your working career and identify the tasks that you loved. Next, make a list of what it was about those tasks that made them so good. What made the time fly? What was it about them that created fond memories?

Part of this might be where you were working or the people with whom you were working. However, part of it will be that you were doing something you loved. That is what you want to capture.

If you're a visual person, you might want to create a timeline of your working life and create a graph marking the highs and lows. It will be your own ECG!

What is it that you're really good at? When you know this, you will be able to work with clients in a way that works for you and them.

Having defined your overall strengths, we're now going to focus on the content of what you do. We're going to talk about your expertise.

Defining your expertise

If you've been working as an employee for someone else, you're likely wanting to stretch your wings and spend more time doing what you love. You have either taken the leap into setting up your own business, or you're sorely tempted.

So what is it that you're so good at that others are going to want to buy you?

Now is not the time to choose to do something completely different from what you have been doing up until now. Where I often see coaches and consultants struggle on start-up is when—fed up with what they are currently doing—they pick an area of 'expertise' that isn't actually their expertise. It's tempting to do this. I've done it myself. You feel slightly jaded towards what has kept your attention in the past, and you see this as an opportunity to try out an area that you've always fancied. Don't do it. If you need a change, change how you work, or with whom you work. Just don't decide to become an overnight expert … well, overnight.

The small business market is awash with consultants and coaches who have decided to be an expert in an area in which, in reality, they are only a few steps ahead of their clients!

This works for a few—the very fast learners, those with enormous self-belief—but my experience has shown that it can take you to a place where you feel that you are always running to catch up. You spend your time on tenterhooks worrying that you're going to be found out that you're not the expert you claim to be! You dread the difficult questions, and you're not ready to move as fast as some of your clients would like.

You become the victim of Imposter Syndrome—when you don't believe that you're really competent at what you are doing, when you think that your success has all been down to chance or luck. Don't let this happen to you. You need, instead, to be knowledgeable, an expert in your field, and you need to know how to get that expertise out there in a way that serves others.

In this chapter I want to define expertise as being about knowledge and skills.

In his book Outliers, Malcolm Gladwell talks about a 10,000-hour rule—the number of hours you need to practice what you do to become an expert. Don't be daunted by this; expert in his reckoning is superstardom, global success—the likes of Bill Gates and the Beatles. What you can take from this, though, is the awareness that the more hours you have spent on skills or knowledge, the more expert you will be.

To declare yourself an expert can feel a little daunting, but it's important on a number of fronts, the most critical of which is that it helps clients really understand what it is you do! It makes you easy to find, easy to understand, and easy to relate to. It means when the time is right, you are the person they pick up the phone and call.

So how will you define your expertise? As I said, it's about skills and/or knowledge.

There will be some obvious links to some of your strengths—if we love doing something, we tend to get really good at it. If you now dig into your skills and knowledge, it will help you create a richer picture of who you are and what you offer. It's key that you know your expertise and that you are comfortable articulating what it is.

Let's get you doing an exercise to get clear on this.

Take out a copy of your CV. Don't worry if it's a bit out of date. It will be good enough to trigger your brain into action.

Now find a piece of paper and run a line down the middle so that you have two columns. Title one column 'Skills' and title the other 'Knowledge'.

At this stage no one else is going to look at this, so just go for it. Work your way through each job you've had and make a note of the skills you developed and the knowledge you gained. Start with your very first job and go right through to today. At this stage write everything that comes to mind; you can edit it later. Don't start picking and choosing!

Write it all down; it will help you get to a place of choice!

Here's a short example:

Skills	Knowledge
Organisation	International marketing
Team management	International education
Communication	Financial services
Project management	French
Politics!	Spanish
Problem solving	Leadership
Writing	

If you come up with a short list, break it down further. What elements of project management were you really good at? You want to define every little skill or every piece of knowledge in which you are an expert. You may be engaged in activities outside work where you've built expertise, so include those too.

Now go through and give each item that you have listed in the two columns a number from 1 to 5 as to how expert you are at it. 1 means not very; 5 means pretty good!

You can now see on what expertise you rate yourself highly. Pull those out onto a separate page and hold onto them. They will be enormously helpful in crafting your marketing message because regardless of whether you choose to be an expert or to niche your business (next chapter!), you are always going to need to be able to explain what it is you do as well as the transformation it brings.

Now that you know your strengths and you're clear on your expertise, it's time to consider who your perfect, potential client is.

Is your business expertise relevant to lots of different types of people or organisations, or is your expertise focused on a very specific, likely very narrow audience?

Let's find out.

Who? – Your perfect potential client

If your focus is to work one-on-one, then the way you approach who you work with is quite different than if you want to work with organisations or with open groups.

Your business can, of course, include a blend of both. For branding purposes, it's smart to have some sort of a connection between the two so that when a client sees both sides of your business, they don't begin to question which one is really you.

Keep in mind, though, being a strategy consultant to organisations whilst coaching people through weight loss might raise an eyebrow for both audiences!

So let's first talk about one-on-one work. Let's talk about niching! This concept has become hugely popular in the coaching world, and you'll see why.

What is a niche? Being literal, it's one of those cute, small alcoves in your house where you would place a precious ornament. That's its root meaning.

When it comes to the coaching world, a niche is about creating a special place in the market where you sit. (Imagine you're the ornament, and you're sitting in your perfect niche, beautifully lit, perfectly set off by your surroundings!) Your niche is likely to be focused on a specific audience and, where possible, offering a specific expertise—the expertise you know you have from doing the exercises in the previous chapter.

Being clear about who your specific audience is means you can target your marketing, your networking, and your promotions to that exact audience, and they can easily see that they are your chosen ones! They can see that you get them, you understand their problems and their challenges, and you know what it is they really want from life!

But before you pick just any niche, there are three questions you must ask yourself to make sure that it's a viable niche that will create a profitable business for you. So, to test this out right now, pick a niche. This may be a type of person or group with whom you've worked before, and it was just easy, fun, or productive. Or it may be a type of person or group you really want to help, so you have great motivation to do so. They may be a niche with whom you feel you have a real affinity, and therefore you feel you will be successful working with them.

Here are the three questions to ask to test the viability of your chosen niche:

Question 1: What is the pain/struggle/problem these people want solved?

If you don't know the answer to this, you need to find it before you start writing any marketing copy and before you approach them. Everyone craves being understood. They want someone who gets where they are stuck and who has the expertise to get them out of that place and to somewhere better!

Question 2: Where can I find 100 of them all in one room?

The point of this question is to check that enough of your clients actually exist and that they flock together. This means you can meet 100 of your perfect, potential clients all in one go! No more searching for the proverbial needle in a haystack.

Question 3: Do they invest in themselves?

There is only one right answer to this question. It has to be a clear 'yes' for you to move forward with this niche. And let me be really clear as to what this question is asking.

It's not asking if they spend money. It is asking if they spend money to develop and create change for themselves—personally.

There are a lot of coaches pushing a lot of niches uphill, hoping that their target group will eventually engage, when, in reality, they are a group that either have never shown signs of personal investment, or they are people with too many other draws on their purse or wallet right now to be able to do something for themselves.

Don't make life hard. Choose a great niche that is going to heave a sigh of relief when they meet you, a niche that are part of a tribe themselves so that you can connect with many of them easily, a niche that is prepared to spend money to get the transformation they crave.

Make sure you pick a niche with whom you really love spending time. That way it will be fun, fulfilling, and feel more like a calling than … well, work.

So does niching work when it comes to organisations?

Frankly, no. Here's why. Yes, organisations like you to understand their industry, market, etc. But they also like to find out what is going on in other industries and markets. We're all curious as to what is going on 'out there', and they will be too.

The paradox is that when you first meet to talk about the possibility of working together, they will ask if you have experience in their sector, so you do need to show some knowledge of what it is they do—an understanding of their scale, the challenges their industry faces, etc. However, you also want to talk to them about what it is you bring because more often than not, it is fresh thinking they are seeking. If you can sprinkle some examples of other organisations you've worked with or in and the transformations you brought about, that will catch their attention.

Through the stories you tell, you will show your expertise. You will help them see clearly that you are someone who will bring the change they are looking for and that you will do it in a way that is unique to you. So if you skipped the expertise chapter, you might want to go back and take a second look.

So how on earth do you decide who you want to work for if organisations are your target market?

There are a couple ways to slice and dice this. Consider the following:

Does it matter what they do? I love working with organisations that do good, that provide a service that improves the life chances for others. These are often in the public or charity sector. I also like working for organisations that have a high street brand, whether that's because of what they do or a product they make. They just make me curious.

Should they be national or international in their market? I like both. If I wasn't working for at least one individual or organisational client that was international, then I'd be out looking for one. Here, it is about what you want and what works for you.

What about the location of the organisation? I remember when I first started out, I was talking to an experienced consultant who 'warned' me that I'd better be prepared to be away from home a lot, on the road the whole time and working long days. Fortunately, he didn't put me off. Sadly, he clearly didn't realise that you can choose just how much of that you do. So consider whether your clients' locations matter. I do work all over the country and also overseas. I just balance that with local clients so that I have time at home to catch up. It's not difficult once you know what it is that works for you.

Finally, with whom would you hate to work? Well, I guess *hate* is strong word, but I'm absolutely sure there will be some sectors or some people that just don't float your boat. Don't pursue them! Whilst you spend time doing things you don't really want to do, you are throwing away time you could spend doing what you do want.

You are now building a really good picture of your business. You know how much you want to work, what will make working a dream for you, what skills and knowledge you will be using, and, from this chapter, you have an idea of who your perfect potential clients might be, whether that's a possible niche of individuals or a sense of a couple industries or markets that you could explore.

Keep these perfect potentials in mind as we move on to consider what it is you're going to offer them so that you have a thriving business.

Your offer

By the end of this chapter, you will have clearly crafted what it is you are offering to perfect, potential clients. But to make that attractive and engaging, there are a few steps to take. You also may need to make a bit of a personal mindset shift to make this easy. If you've come out of a corporate environment, please understand that this chapter is essential.

To put it bluntly, you are no longer going to be recognised for your expertise. (I know—I've just done a whole chapter on expertise, but stay with me.) You will be recognised for the positive impact you have on others, and to do that you need to talk about transformation.

From the previous chapters, you've gathered lots of really great information about you, and you are now in a great place to begin to craft your offer.

You know what your sweet spot is, you can define your expertise, and you know who your perfect, potential clients are.

Let's take all of that and put it into the melting pot for you to craft the message that is your offer.

The key here is for you to get used to moving away from talking about expertise to talking about transformation. You also want to let go of making an offer that is based on what you think your potential, perfect client needs. It must be based on what they want!

Let me give you an example.

Someone with whom I've worked for many years took the exciting step of starting up a consultancy practice. They booked a ninety-minute strategy session with me to get clear on what it is they wanted to offer. Their expertise is in corporate social responsibility (CSR) with some sustainability thrown in.

They were clear on their target audience, but what they hadn't considered was how their target audience would benefit from the service they offered. Not only that, but they also hadn't considered why on earth they would spend precious resources to hire a consultant with this expertise.

This wasn't about selling CSR. The title itself has been used so often I personally think it has lost its meaning a bit. This needed to be about selling what would happen if they became socially responsible.

After a bit of a grilling—albeit reasonably gentle grilling—we were able to come up with the transformation that would come about through an organisation being more socially responsible. For example, there are significant resource efficiencies to be had (NB: money is always a great trigger for any client), their profile and reputation would be greatly enhanced, it could open up opportunities to do business with new clients, and from a hiring perspective, it could be a great sales tool when it came to hiring new millennials.

Then we talked about why these organisations weren't just getting on with it themselves. It turns out

CSR is complex to start up and even more complex—and time-consuming—to integrate. It is the complexity of it all that keeps them awake at night and puts them off making that first step.

We now had a whole different set of information to use to attract clients. So what was going to make them sit up and take notice of this particular consultant over her competitors?

She has to offer a service that helps organisations:

- create a reputation as a place where you want to do business
- open up new markets
- appeal to the new generation of employees who see CSR as a fundamental part of business
- create significant resource efficiencies
- make sense of something complex
- integrate CSR in a way that doesn't take the focus off the day to day running of the business

Now she was in a really good place to go out to a few perfect, potential clients and test which of these really resonated. What was important was to discover which ones created a 'tell me more' reaction. Those would become the offer.

You might be thinking, 'I'm able offer lots of different things to clients'. I get you. My world is all about leadership. Can you imagine how many different offers can spin off that? However, at this stage, and with new clients, you want to have a core offer, one that gets you in the door to start a great relationship. Once you've achieved that, you are able to offer more. I cover this later in the book when I cover engagement.

So let's take a look at you.

You have great skills, great knowledge, and tools to draw on that you know are perfect for the job. But that's not what you want to shout about. You want to tell people about the change you make—the transformation you bring—when they work with you.

Before you even start on this, ask yourself if you know what your perfect, potential client wants. And if you know what they want, do you know why they want it? Do they know why they want it?!

If you can't answer this, go out and do a bit of research. Go to the places where they get together. Join some online groups to see what help they are looking for. Really listen to what they say and the words they use. Capture these. One of the key reasons I offer strategy sessions for free is that it provides me with rich data that helps me understand where my audience are at.

Please find out what is keeping them awake. Be tenacious in asking the 'Why?' questions. Use the simple marketing exercise 'The 5 Whys' to help you, and then, dig deeper. This exercise is very simple. You ask them why, and when they give you the answer, ask them why again and do it 5 times. Don't worry—it's not as irritating as it sounds, and they will thank you for helping them think!

Also, always find out why they haven't done

anything yet about solving their problem, achieving their goals, etc. If they have tried before, find out why it didn't work. The way you work (your strengths) might be just what they need.

When you understand your client's wants, when you understand why they want it and why they aren't doing anything about it, you can then create an offer that meets their needs. It is then that you turn into a magnet!

Work your way through the grid below to craft your offer.

My perfect, potential client is

_____

What they want is

_____

Five reasons they want this are:

1.

2.

3.

4.

5.

They struggle to achieve this because

_____

They stay awake at night worrying because

_____

To give you an example, here's my offer grid completed:

My perfect potential client is someone who is ready and excited about setting up their own coaching/consulting practice.

They want it to be a success without burning out.

Five reasons they want this are:

1. They want to make really good money—more than they have in the past.
2. They want the freedom that working for themselves brings.
3. They want to take what they are passionate about out into the world.
4. They want to be able to balance work and life and make the most of both.
5. They want to be able to work with clients they love.

They struggle to achieve this because they are feeling overwhelmed as to where to start.

They stay awake at night worrying they will have to go back into employment and never realise their dreams.

Now you can see why I wrote Get Clients 101!

My offer focuses on helping new coaches and consultants (and even some experienced ones) transform their expertise into a powerful and profitable client-getting business that is high value, has high integrity, and is done with elegance and ease.

Get your offer crafted, and then let's move on because now you are ready to work out just how many of those clients you need!

How many clients do you need?

Though you might be thinking the opposite, answering just this one question can greatly reduce your feelings of being overwhelmed when you look at building your business.

Your answer, which you'll have once you've worked through what follows, is going to help you set a really clear *Get Clients 101* goal. It will help you get super focused on who to approach, you will be able to track progress as you build your empire, and the really good news is you probably don't need as many as you think.

To be able to answer this question you will need to draw on your answers to the two questions posed earlier in this book about how much time you want to spend working and how much you want to earn. This is where you begin to get real clarity.

So how do you work out how many clients?

Some people like working with lots of new clients all the time because the idea of repeat business and working with the same people isn't attractive to them. If you are one of these people, you need to work through this chapter with a focus on creating an annual target for yourself that takes into account that each year you're starting from scratch.

An alternative model is to have some new clients each year, but also to have a strong focus on creating repeat business. I personally really value this model for several reasons. First, you get to do much broader work with each client as the relationship grows. Second, there are fewer sales cycles to start off and fathom your way through. Third, as you develop a relationship, you also develop the opportunities for them to refer you to new clients (even fewer sales cycles!).

Regardless of which model you prefer, keep in mind that you want to include associate work in the mix. I'll talk more about this in a later chapter. For now, what I mean by this is being an associate consultant or coach for a consulting firm. They win the work and then get associates to deliver it—you being one of those associates.

But here and now, let's focus on you getting your own clients.

First: Get out your notebook or scrap of paper or whatever it was you were using when you were dreaming about how much time you want to spend working and how much you'd like to earn.

Second: From the previous chapter, what are you going to offer? Do you currently want to do one-on-one work, which would **mean** you'll likely offer coaching packages? Or will you work with organisations, which could mean anything from two days to more than twenty-five days a year. Will you have associate work? Start off with some random ideas, and then see what it looks like in respect to your time/money calculations. Note that by the time you finish this book, you will have learned lots of different ways to work with clients and you can come back and do this again.

For the time being, let me give you an example of working out your 'how many':

You like the idea of having six one-on-one coaching clients per year.

They are going to be on a six-month programme, and for that programme you're going to charge around 4,000 per client. So a quick calculation tells you your revenue for this will be 24,000. I doubt very much this is what you're hoping to earn! But now double it. Let's say you work with twelve clients a year. Now you're looking at 48,000.

Maybe you also want to do some consultancy work with a few organisations. Let's be conservative and say that you deliver a workshop that goes down well, and you're asked back to do more. (I've been delivering the same coaching skills workshop for a client for over three years now—it's a large organisation!) For that one client you are now delivering six days a year. So let's say that at around a conservative day rate of 800, plus the couple days' design time as well as delivery to be charged, you've now added 6,400 to your revenue stream.

You speak to another prospective client about what you are doing, and they ask you to do something similar, but they need a series of different workshops and each needs design. This means another twelve days of work and another 9,600.

Your revenue is now at 64,000 with twelve individual coaching clients and two organisational clients. Depending on the design of your platinum (six-month) programmes, you're probably working about seventy billable days a year.

If your plan is to do a four-day week, then even if you were using fifty days a year as non-billable business building time, you would still have another fifty days to play around with!

Really think about what you have discovered in the last few chapters and spend some time thinking about your answer to this question regarding how many clients you need.

This is both fun and really useful, and you can access the *Get Clients 101* Income Stream Calculator on the site to help make this super easy to do. I give you some additional revenue streams to consider there, and you can see how your year would look.

It's surprisingly easy to create a plan to get to six figures and above, which leads me to your final step.

Third. How much do you charge?

I've given you some conservative day rates above. But here's the truth. What you charge will vary enormously. I'd love to be able to say to you, 'This is how much', but it's just not that simple.

There are a number of factors, many of which you will not be able to influence, apart from with whom you choose to work. These are:

- Industry sector
- The type of work you do
- The level of your audience (the more senior they are, the higher the pay)

If you do associate work, your rate will be fixed by the consultancy who commissioned you, and they are likely to bill the client significantly more than the rates I've mentioned here. They have their own overheads to cover, so don't get in a tizz about that.

Make the most of your network and ask around about rates. Few people publish them, but you might occasionally find the information tucked away somewhere online. Be prepared: organisations will pay anything from 400 to 1,500+. Using the Get Client 101 Income Stream Calculator, you will be able to see the impact that different day rates will have.

So in truth, to be able to answer the 'how many client do I really need' question, all you have to remember is who, how often, and how much?

Now that you know how many you want to work with and that you're not talking hundreds, you should be feeling confident about getting out and finding them. So let's talk visibility next.

Visibility

You now have everything you need to get out there. You know who you want to meet and what it is they want. You're clear on what you have to offer, so now all you need to do is find your perfect, potential clients and get in front of them.

I hope that if you're someone who, before you picked up this book, loathed the idea of 'networking', you're beginning to feel that it might not be quite so bad since you've worked your way through the first six chapters.

In this chapter we're going to look at how to get you visible in a way that works for both you and potential clients. I'm intentionally avoiding talking about social media at this stage. That will come later. Why? It can be a real time drain, and we have to remember that people buy people. If you're in the service business and you're a one-person band, people are buying you, and the quickest way for them to make a decision to work with you is to meet you.

Always keep in mind that potential clients do business with people they know, like, and trust. So you want to constantly look for ways to connect with people so that they can find out more about you. You want to connect in ways and in places where you can be yourself and where you can build the opportunity for multiple connections that will build trust.

There is no point in having great expertise and

fantastic skills if you have no one to work with. And I see this a little too often—great coaches and consultants who are struggling—whilst on the other side of the coin, coaches and consultants who aren't particularly great have a full diary and great income. The difference between the two is their mindset about getting visible. It can be fun!

I want to split this section into two, depending on whether you are focusing your business on individuals or on organisations. I'd advise going about it in different ways. If you're doing a bit of both, then split your time accordingly.

Let's start with finding individual clients. Remember as you read this to keep your niche and what they want in mind so that it makes sense. How can you network effectively to get clients?

When I started out, I attended hundreds of networking events over the first few years, never with any real sense of purpose and always with a very poor return on investment of my time.

I've done everything from the crazy early morning breakfast sessions to the expensive members only, posh hotel sessions, and a whole lot of others in between. I had some nice food and met some nice people, but to be honest, it got me absolutely nowhere. My mistake was I hadn't established my perfect, potential client, so I wasn't hanging out with them in large numbers. Instead, I was doing the needle in the haystack search—and rarely finding a needle.

Using networking to discover and connect with potential clients is perfect if you are networking with your niche. Let's take a simple example.

You provide a specific service to accountants.

Remember, they have to know, like, and trust you, so how will you build those factors in the accounting world?

First, you know a bit about this audience. Where do they meet (professional bodies tend to have get-togethers)? What do they read? Who else is a trusted resource that they go to for advice or guidance? Who do you know personally in that world and with whom could you have a chat? Who, if they know you well and have a good understanding of what you do (and only if that is the case), could make some introductions for you?

What opportunities might there be for you to speak to this audience of accountants? If that sounds daunting, it doesn't have to be an audience of 100. It could be a local group that gets together once a month, and you could take along '10 tips to . . .' to share. Standing up and speaking to a group is an instant way for them to see you as an expert. Make sure you get contact details and do great follow-up with a strategy session or the like so that you can connect personally. When I've been a speaker, I have never gotten less than 80 percent of the group's contact details.

Is there a publication for whom you could offer to write an article? Remember, if you know where your audience is stuck, you are likely to have your hand bitten off if you offer content that helps get them unstuck!

Create two or three topics that you could speak/write about, and get in touch with group organisers and editors and offer them a choice of titles. Seeing which one they choose is super useful in itself.

One of my favourite ways of meeting people is at conferences, particularly those that include interactive workshops or breakouts. Why? One, because I get to learn something, and two, if there are scheduled opportunities to interact, I'm going to get a chance to make a great connection with a group of new people. As always, make sure you stay connected! They will have gotten to know you, and they may like you, but it's consistent connection that creates the trust.

So there are some tips for getting visible for individual clients. But what about organisations?

This takes a very different approach. This is when *who* you know really matters. This is also when having associate work in your revenue streams is gold, on a number of fronts. More on that in the next section.

To make it easy to get organisational work, you need to have a great referral network. This can be made up of a number of different types of people. Keep in mind that you don't need lots of different organisations to keep your diary filled. Working really well with a few is likely to be enough.

So who do you need in that referral network?

You need people who know you well and understand what you do. Don't ignore the latter part of that last sentence. It does you no good to have a bunch of friends who are happy to tell everyone about you if they are not educated in using your transformation statement—albeit scripted in a way that sounds natural to them. Make sure they know what you're up to, your success stories, etc.

You need people you have worked with in the past. This works well if the work you're doing is similar to the work you were doing when you knew them. If you're doing something very different, they may not be such a perfect fit as they may not be clear themselves as to what it is you actually do.

You need other coaches and consultants. This is a rich seam, and the great thing is it's reciprocal. Looking at this on the surface, you may think this group are your competitors, and I guess in a way they are.

However, they are also really well connected to various organisational projects. I would calculate that at least half the organisational work I've done has come through colleagues who are consultants and/or coaches who have put me forward as someone else to be on the team. I've even had people hand me their clients because they are moving out of the field or because they have other work that is using up their time and attention. Networking amongst peers is very, very valuable. And there will be a time when a client asks you for someone with a certain specialty, and if you can refer someone great to them, that means lots of brownie points for you!

Having associate work—when you carry out work on behalf of a consultancy on a freelance basis—will give you the opportunity to meet some other great coaches and consultants, and they will likely end up being a great support network of friends and colleagues.

The final referral group is clients with whom you have already worked. There is a time and place for when it's suitable to ask for a referral. They need to have reached that 'know, like, trust' place, and I'd suggest you request it just after you've delivered something fabulous! Some clients might not want to refer you to others in the same sector, and you shouldn't expect your clients to come up with who they should refer you to. Make it easy for them. Check out who they are likely to know and then specifically ask for an introduction to be made.

So you have plenty to do now.

Tap into your niche audience, find out where they meet, and go join them. Please summon up the courage to offer to speak. You will be delighted with the results.

Look through your diary and your online connections. Seek out those who know you well, and think about who they could introduce you to.

This isn't difficult. It's about making a plan, and now that you know who your potential, perfect client is, you now know how to go about connecting with them.

This chapter completes the section about foundations.

From here on out you can be out there, feeling confident about who you are and what you are offering, making some great connections, and most importantly turning those connections into clients and creating a flourishing business to be proud of.

Now I want us to move into the phase of creating revenue streams. It's time to have some fun with the way you work with clients, ways that you and they love and that are great for business.

Having a revenue-streams mindset is hugely valuable. It gives you variety, broadens who you work with and how you work with them, and most importantly creates business resilience if the markets gets rocky.

.

REVENUE STREAMS

'Abundance is not something we acquire. It is something we tune into.'

– Wayne Dwyer

Your foundations are now in place, and you're clear about what you're offering and to whom. Now we're going to take a look at how you can create multiple revenue streams without getting into a place filled with long hours, a place that would overwhelm you.

In this section I'm going to divide who you work with into individuals, organisations, and consultancies (your associate work). Then I want to talk about products—often unrealistically positioned as passive income, which isn't quite true.

When you look at your business as a collection of revenue streams, it will become clear where you need to focus, what you need to prioritise, and basically where you'll get the best bang for your buck, which is all about knowing which clients produce the best revenue for the time you spend with them. This will tell you what you need to do more, and, frankly, what to stop doing!

Right now I want to focus on the different ways you can choose to work with clients.

Specific content design ideas will be covered in the next section when I talk about empowering clients.

Individuals

Let's start with a revenue stream that is coaching individuals one-on-one. I want to be totally honest. Working one-on-one, face-to-face, using the traditional one or two-hour session coaching model is great, but unless your clients have lots of money, live next door to you, and you both have lots of free diary space, it's not easy!

It can seem straightforward, but struggling to find times in the diary that work, which then get cancelled at the last minute, is incredibly frustrating. Also, if you're travelling to meet clients, it can be difficult to get enough clients booked in one day to generate enough income to take coaching from hobby to business. It's one of the reasons that coaching sessions end up with a high price tag.

'But lots of people want to work face-to-face!' you cry. I know! So you have to design a way to work that delivers high-value services to your coaching clients, a way that enables them to see you as accessible that also keeps you from having to struggle to keep your diary filled.

So how do you work with an individual in a way that builds a great relationship, that allows them to experience the transformation you bring, and that helps you work together over a long enough period of time that they achieve their goals?

Consider it a step-by-step process. Most coaches these days offer some sort of discovery/strategy sessions, and more often than not, these are free. This is a smart move. You remember me talking about the 'know, like, trust' factor? This is a great first step towards building that. These sessions should focus on getting your perfect, potential client really clear on what it is they want and what's getting in the way. These sessions should not be designed to give them all the answers (an easy trap to fall into); otherwise, there would be no reason to sign up to work with you, and there also would be no way to ensure the client's problem/challenge/goal had been properly scoped.

The potential client gets value from the clarity the session brings, and you get the opportunity to share ways that you could help them move forward if they were to work with you.

That's all great. They love the session and they want to work with you. What next?

Please don't just sign them up to a string of coaching sessions! I've done this in the past. It starts off with great momentum, but it can so easily splutter and fade. And I don't think it sounds that exciting, does it?

What you want to do is offer them an opportunity to work with you over a three- to six-month period. You need to know how you will use this time so that they will achieve the transformation they crave.

What's great is the programme length gives the coaching relationship parameters. You will provide them with the steps they will take during this period, you will get the programme booked into both your diaries, and (the best thing of all) you will have the chance to provide a blended learning experience, which means the process will be a mixture of face-to-face, telephone, and offline learning.

Remember, if someone is feeling stuck, they will be feeling confused, probably overwhelmed, and unsure what to do next. You come along and offer them a clearly structured five-step programme to move them from stuck to success. They can see the journey ahead, and they can see that it's one step at a time. Everything suddenly seems possible.

Let me share with you the structure of one of the three- to six-month programmes I offer to clients. I may change the steps slightly, depending on where the client is and where they want to go, but the way I deliver and connect with them stays the same.

- They receive my leadership strengths profiling tool. This helps me understand their preferences and gives me insight into what they might find difficult to do going forward. I also get insight into what motivates them so that I can help make the transformation easier.
- We book a direction/action setting day in the diary there and then. This is a day spent together in person or virtually, depending on their circumstances/geographical location. A good dose of face-to-face interaction builds trust quickly. This day is designed to take them through a journey. (Ways to map out this journey are covered in a few chapters' time.)
- Each month they can draw down on two forty-five-minute coaching sessions—by phone.
- At the midpoint we meet for another direction/action session, this time for a half day.

(The coaching sessions will inform the exact focus.)

• The programme finishes with a final day together.

In addition to this, I gift them with a number of different items, including a workbook, e-mail access, and some self-directed learning modules.

I hope you can see how this creates a time-bound, structured programme with clear milestones and strong, regular connection. You can adjust this design to your clients and their availability, but keep the sense of progress, make sure you have designed the time well that you spend together, and use the forty-five-minute coaching sessions as the glue that keeps the motivation to transform firmly in place.

I've spent the majority of this chapter talking about working with individuals one-on-one as I think that is how many coaches like to work. However, there are other options that you could consider, such as small group masterminds. I'd suggest somewhere between four and six participants so that everyone gets quality time and attention from you, or open workshops that you market to individuals. Just make sure you give yourself at least three months' lead time to fill those places!

However, if you choose to work with clients one-on-one, remember that adults learn by doing, not by being told what to do. I present more ideas on this in the empowering clients section.

That is one-on-one work explored. Now what could you do with organisations?

Organisations

Well, the world is your oyster when it comes to different ways of working with organisations. Since we're talking revenue streams, let's think about ways that work fantastically for clients and that also make the most of your time.

I'm going to group this section into three areas: coaching, consulting, and workshops. If you work with organisations, you're likely to be constantly moving in and out of these areas and often combining the skills and knowledge needed in all three.

Coaching

In the last chapter I talked about 'programmatising' coaching, which is to say creating a stepped process when working with one-on-one clients. It's a mindset that is worth keeping when it comes to coaching inside organisations. The difference is an organisational client is less likely to want to take a day or half a day out of their calendar. Instead, you might want to consider doing a two-hour strategy session up front on how you will work together and what key topics you will cover, and then move into an agreed series of coaching sessions with all the additional learning pieces scattered through the period. The more you diarise and the more consistently the sessions are held, the more success you will have.

Other ways to use your coaching expertise are:

Team coaching – This is very similar to facilitation, so make sure your clients understand the difference. I really like team coaching. There's little or no preparation up front—maybe just a quick briefing call with the team's leader and then you show up and coach. Having the opportunity to showcase your coaching skills can lead to one-on-one coaching, so it's a nice seeding activity. (Seeding will be covered in more depth in a few chapters' time.)

Coaching clinics – I love doing these. Some coaches get a bit bent out of shape when asked to do them because they can't charge their normal hourly rate, but if you follow my one-on-one model, you don't have an hourly rate anyway! I often offer these to clients as, again, it gives me the chance to use a skill I love, and it spreads the word about coaching and the value of it across the organisation. I usually do six sessions a day and charge a day's consultancy rate. Yes, that will make some people squeal that it's cheap, but the value added to the organisation is high, and the connections I make internally are priceless. It's a guaranteed way to increase the work you do with organisations.

Consulting

If you're a coach reading this and you don't see yourself as a consultant, take another look. You would make a great one! Consulting for me is all about the value added using diagnostics, creating great interventions, and really getting under the skin of a company. It's about helping an organisation, or sometimes an individual, understand why they are where they are and then giving advice and guidance as to how to move forward.

Individual diagnostics – There are plenty of personality profiling tools out there, such as the Myers

Briggs Type Indicator, etc. But if you are asking people to reflect on themselves, whether that's through rating themselves or answering questions about themselves, you can prepare simple self-diagnostics yourself.

Organisational diagnostics – This might be designing and carrying out interviews, running workshops to surface employee issues, creating and sending out questionnaires, and collating and feeding back the data gathered. The likes of surveymonkey.com provide easy and cost-effective ways to do this. When you first start working with an organisation, always try to do some of this up front so that you get a sense of the organisation. You will also get to meet some of the staff, which will put you in good stead for any further work with them.

Creating some simple diagnostic tools around your expertise gives you a richer offer to make to your perfect, potential client and forms part of an attractive package to offer them (more about this in the next section).

Once you understand what is going on, it's so much easier to design the right next steps. That might be workshops, it might be focusing on a specific area or team, it might be coaching, or it might be some straightforward engagement on getting people to learn something new.

Workshops

Organisations love workshops. I really enjoy delivering workshops, but my concern is always that they are a bit of a one-hit wonder. People show up, have an enjoyable day, but actually put very little of what they learn into practice. (The apocryphal statistic is around 20 percent of the learning actually gets used, but personally I think it's less.) Add to that the research telling us that humans can concentrate for around five hours maximum, and a whole day can sound like too much. But as I said, organisations love them, so having a selection of different topics on which you can run workshops is a smart part of your revenue stream. Where you can add real value and increase that percentage of learning is how you top and tail the workshops (again, more about this in the next section— as well as how interactive you can make them).

Workshops can last anywhere from two hours to several days. If you're asked to run a two-hour learning bite, offer to run two or three in one day so that your time is used well.

All workshops need design time. The standard rule is one to one and a half days of design per each day of delivery. However, if you do create a two-hour session, I would suggest charging a half day as there can be just as much pre- and post-prep as for a normal one-day workshop.

Those are the three broad ways that you can engage with an organisation. Within those three are hundreds of different topics you could cover, and many different ways to work with your clients. Use your intuition and listen to what they are telling you they need, and you won't go far wrong.

Associate work

There are many different ways to boost your

business revenue, create a bit of stability, and do really interesting work, but none beats becoming an associate with a consulting company for achieving all three things in one go—and quickly.

Including associate work as one of your revenue streams is a really smart move.

I know quite a few people who, when they first started out, were adamant that they weren't running a proper business unless they had their own clients. I get that; it's good to feel you're running your own business. They were so keen to break the shackles of being—and feeling—employed by someone else that they couldn't face working freelance as an associate for a consultancy. However, the benefits are huge, and it's a trick not to be missed.

First up though, if you're just stepping into creating your own coaching/consulting business, you may want to know what I mean by associate work.

Many consultancies, large and small, use consultants on an as- and when-needed basis. I'm going to use the word 'consultant' through this chapter, but this applies equally to you if you are a coach. (I get a lot of coaching work through my associate relationships.)

If you're reading this and thinking, 'My expertise is around lifestyle issues. I don't think organisations are that interested', I'd suggest thinking again. As more and more attention is being given to health, stress, work/life balance, mindfulness, etc., I think these areas will become more mainstream. You just have to help potential, prospective clients see the very clear link between lifestyle and successful business, and research and data are the keys here.

Consultancies work in different ways when it comes to creating project teams. Some might have a core group of consultants as full-time employees and back-fill bigger projects with associates. Other consultancies— particularly the boutique ones—tend to have their entire team on an associate model. It gives them the flexibility to draw on whichever skill set each project needs.

There are three clear advantages to adding associate work into the mix that is your business:

- If you don't like selling, this is a way to get work without doing any sales. Consultancies tend to lead on the sales and then put associates onto the projects once the business is won.
- You get to work with large clients who wouldn't contemplate working with a sole provider, which is great when it comes to impressing your own clients. You are therefore likely to work on potentially more interesting and complex projects. My international work has always come through my associate revenue stream.
- You get to work in a team. This is something that I love about associate work. I don't mind working on my own, but it's also great to work with other people, share ideas, come up with new designs, find out what the latest research is and how others are using it, and to be honest, just being around other people who are peers is always good.

Associate work isn't difficult to find. But before you hit the net or the phones, write yourself a decent bio and insert a good picture of yourself. Then you'll be able to respond quickly to anyone who is interested in you. (Download a bio template at *getclients101.com/toolkit.*) I work only with boutique consultancies simply because that's my preference, but I know from colleagues that the steps I give you below work for the larger firms too.

It's tempting to present yourself as a generalist in your field, but I'd counsel that it's better to offer the skills, knowledge, and expertise that you love using. It also helps whoever allocates work in the consultancy to see where you might fit on certain projects.

So how do you create couple great associate relationships? In over ten years of running my established business, I've worked consistently with three consultancies. That has been more than enough to keep my associate revenue stream full. It's the usual story: being good at what you do—which you are—means that work will flow your way.

The steps are simple.

1. Get clear on what it is you have to offer. Having a niche skill as a consultant can work very well; after all, you can have associate relationships with more than one consultancy. You could be attractive to a consultancy from a number of different perspectives: who you worked for in the past (whether that's brand or sector), the level at which you've operated, who you're connected to, and finally and obviously what it is you're really good at.

   Remember to talk about transformation and results.

2. Research the types of consultancies that you think could use your expertise, which is really easy to do online. Check that they have an associate team. (You'll always find them on the 'about us' type of page.) Does it look like it's a fit for you? For me, the values of the company are the most critical thing. I've turned down invitations to join associate teams because I haven't liked the way they do business!

When I first started up, I just got on the web and searched for consultancies working in the field of leadership and organizational development who clearly already had associates on their books.

Give them a call to see if they would be interested in someone with your background and skillset. You may find some are one-person bands posing as a larger outfit, but don't be put off. One of the first calls I made was to a company with whom I still work today. Calling is important as it will give you a sense of what they are like, and it creates a really quick connection.

3. Talk to other coaches and consultants about who they are working with. (The absolute quickest way to become an associate is to be recommended by a current team member. You can be on a project within a week!)

If this makes you feel a bit nervous, don't be. The smart consultancies are always willing to talk to good consultants. I say this from having been the manager of a consultancy team a while back. When you run a consultancy, you always want great people on your team, and you always keep a lookout for them.

You'll no doubt come across a lot of consultants who work 100 percent as associates, and as long as there is work out there, it can make for an easy and enjoyable life.

As you gain experience and create new relationships, you'll quickly discover which consultancies are a great fit for you and which ones aren't. In my experience, a good fit entails a very trusting relationship where you have plenty of leeway to do what you think is right. It exposes you to clients and locations you might never be able to access through your own business, it gives you an opportunity to meet great new colleagues in your field, and it provides you with a relatively stable income stream.

However you choose to design your business, associate work is a revenue stream you want to embrace.

Let's now move on to a different type of revenue stream—products!

Products

You've now got a business that is all about serving your clients brilliantly. However, it's currently a business where if you're not in front of someone or on the phone to them, you're not earning money. Your business relies heavily on you being present to earn money—and that's fine. You can have a very successful business just sticking with this model.

The good news is that it is also the perfect foundation for you to begin to integrate products as an additional revenue stream.

By 'products' I mean something you create once and sell multiple times. There will be up-front design time, and it's likely to be a lot of time. But once the product is designed, your time can be spent on other things. It also means that clients don't have to pay bespoke design fees every time they work with you, so it's a win-win for both sides.

There's one caveat I would put out there about this type of revenue stream. Many see products as an opportunity to create passive income, or 'money on the beach' as it is sometimes referred, implying that once the product is up, money starts to pour in. It's marketing hype.

You might not spend a lot of time constantly designing or delivering fresh material, but what you will do is spend that time marketing and selling so that you drive perfect, potential clients to purchase it. Products become truly, stratospherically profitable when you are able to reach tens of thousands of people—and I'm not going to cover that sort of marketing in this book.

But don't despair. There are still some lovely opportunities for products to be added as a great revenue stream to build your business, and what is great is products can extend your client reach. If you start with this mindset thinking, 'How can I turn "this" (whatever 'this' is that you are currently doing in person) into a product?' it will serve you well as you expand your empire!

Let's look at what I mean by 'products'.

Types of products:

Workbooks – Workbooks can be great add-on purchases to those attending workshops. They provide them with some next steps, words of advice, and a place to track progress. They need to be designed well and produced to a certain level of quality to attract people to purchase them.

Profiling tools – We all love to learn more about ourselves, so depending on what it is you are helping others with, it's great to have a tool that helps them understand more about themselves. I created a leadership profiling tool so that clients can see why they love doing some of their tasks, but hate others. I see other tools out there that help people understand happiness, stress, work/life balance, etc. Make it something easy and fun to use so that people engage quickly.

Books/eBooks – These are clearly a little more static and create less engagement, but books can be both valuable to clients and a door opener for you. Despite this being the era of self-publishing and everyone becoming an author, there is still some credibility to be had for being an author. Books that take the reader through a number of steps or a process that creates a map for them are always popular.

Audio downloads – This can be another great add-on to work you are currently doing. They are easy to create and simple to upload onto a site or pop on a memory stick to build on topics that you have already delivered. Clients will welcome anything that is portable because it means they can access it when it works for them. Audio is particularly good for this as it can be listened to on the way home, whether on a train or in a car.

Remember, whatever you create must be really easy to access and straightforward to use.

Despite—or maybe because of—the ease of access to information via the web, people seem to really like receiving parcels through the mail, so don't feel that you have to be a tech wizard to create these things. However, you should focus on the look and feel of the product ('face validity' as it's known in psychological circles).

Yes, the content has to be good, but people also need to be excited when they receive your products too. First impressions count.

So, I've covered the *what*. Let's take a look at the *how*.

Get a big piece of paper.

Start with being clear on what your expertise is and write that in the middle. Then brainstorm all the different topics you could cover that fall under the umbrella of what it is you do.

When you've got ten or more topics on your sheet of paper, consider which ones you know people would be interested in. If you're not sure, talk to current clients about which ones they would like to have access to. You always, always want to be designing to what people want.

Once you've decided on a couple topics, think about how you will productise them. Will they work best as a workbook, a series of audios, or maybe even both?

How will they fit neatly into what you already do so that you can let your clients know they are there for them, that they are additional steps they can take on their journey of development?

How will people know about them and access them? Do you have opportunities to talk about them when you are out and about? Do you have a client list that you can market to?

Selling products to strangers takes time; remember the 'know, like, trust' factor. People aren't likely to spend money with someone they know nothing about. There is an art to this method of marketing, and a lot of it has to do with selling something people can't live without—or making them feel they can't live without it! It's also about the price point at which you offer a product. People will experiment with the unknown when the cost is low, but are less likely to splash out when it is high.

So remember, if you've just run a great workshop,

then you have a willing audience who will want to dig deeper and do more, and you can offer an additional product to them.

There are more opportunities for products in the virtual world, and I'll talk about this much later. For now, get used to the idea of creating products from the content you have, and play around with creating something that your clients will love.

EMPOWER YOUR CLIENT

'As we seek to discover the best in others, we somehow bring out the best in ourselves.'

– William Arthur Ward

Client mindset

When you empower your client, you empower yourself.

You can't take a horse to water and make it drink. The same can be said for a client. Your client must have the mindset of wanting to change and move forward. Your client must be excited—and yes, possibly even a bit daunted—at the journey ahead, but they must want it!

What happens if they don't? Then you will spend time in an unsatisfactory working relationship that will frustrate and disappoint you both. It will feel like hard work, you will dread seeing their name on your calendar as your next appointment, and at the end of your time with them, you will feel unfulfilled and fed up!

As human beings we quickly absorb the energy of others, so you owe it to them and yourself to make sure that whenever you work together, you are doing so really effectively. That's why they need to come to you ready for change.

This starts from the first time you connect.

If people didn't feel stuck in life or didn't have grand ambitions to move forward, there would be no work for coaches. However, when people are in that stuck place or don't know what their next steps are, they can feel frustrated and vent that frustration on you! Venting is fine, but it needs to be done within boundaries, so let's look at ways that you can invite them into a space of moving forward constructively—and together.

Discover/strategy sessions

It's become commonplace for discovery/strategy sessions to be the first real experience you and your perfect, potential client have to work together. They are still a potential client at this stage, so remember you are using the session to give them a sense of what working with you is like. This session is about getting clarity—not finding solutions. For that reason alone it is the perfect place to begin to empower them.

There are different views about the best way to run strategy sessions (as I call them). I strongly counsel you not to use them as one almighty sales pitch. It's off-putting at best; at worst, you talk someone into working with you who might not be a great fit.

Begin the session letting them know how long it will take—I usually say thirty to forty-five minutes. Be clear that you want to dig deeper to help them get clarity and that, only if it seems appropriate and only at their request, you will share how you work with clients to achieve their goals at the very end of the session.

Use the time to explore and connect your client to their dream, whether it's building an amazing business, losing weight, sleeping better at night, or finding the perfect partner!

By connecting them emotionally to their desire, you *both* discover just how important this is.

Secondly, you then want to unearth where they are right now. You want to find out what that feels like and what is keeping them in that place. Is it about physical or mental obstacles? Is there a belief or lack of belief that is getting in their way? Dig down to help them.

Finally, make a couple key observations based on what you've heard. Play those observations back to them to help them understand what is going on. Use your intuition, and if needs be, be gentle.

Finish the session by asking if they would like to hear about how you could help them achieve their dream. Then wait and let them step into that place called accountability, where they get to choose if they want to move forward—or not.

Always be prepared for them to say yes (that shouldn't be a surprise!) so that you can run smoothly into the next steps.

But before we get into that, make sure you've taken really great notes—ideally verbatim notes (avoiding any sort of summarizing that changes the language). This first strategy session is the anchor for the rest of the time you work together. It's your stake in the ground. As you move forward, you will be able to refer back to it to show them how far they have come, how their mindset has shifted, and how much they have achieved. I am still in touch with a client that I worked with several years ago, and every time we speak we refer in some way back to where he was when we first met and how far he has come. It's wonderful to be able to reflect on that place.

Now, back to the more practical and pragmatic elements of this first connection. Your client wants to believe that everything will run smoothly. They want to feel confident in you, and they want to understand how and when you will work together. So be ready to show them that you've thought of all that too! Stumbling around at this sensitive point will be like popping a balloon.

Be ready to share how the programme will work going forward. Be ready to book dates in your diaries. Be clear on their payment options—is it all up front? Can they pay in two parts? Is it monthly? Make sure you know the numbers! If you make it smooth and easy, their confidence levels will remain high.

Contract

Remember, this is a business relationship, and your clients will appreciate you being businesslike about it. Once they've agreed to work with you, send them a simple contract to be signed and returned. (Download a basic contract to get you started at *getclients101.com/toolkit.*)

The point of the contract is to set boundaries, whether that's being clear about what happens if one of you can't make a meeting or a call, or whether it answers questions in their head around confidentiality.

From a mindset perspective, a contract makes working together real! It also, if needs be, gives you somewhere to connect back to if things start to get flabby! You know what I mean.

The basics are sorted. You likely have your first meeting scheduled, so what can you have them do in the meantime that keeps them connected to their dream, with a mindset of possibility?

It's simple—have something prepared that you can

send them immediately, whether that's something to read, a profiling tool that will create insight for them, or a questionnaire to complete. Just make sure it's the right first step for where they are starting from, and point out the value of it for them.

Make sure it engages them. (If it's an article, ask what they will take away from it.) And make sure it's something that gives them insight into why it was such a good idea to work with you!

You're all set. Let's now make sure you don't confuse what you think they need with what they want—or at least, let's seamlessly weave the two together.

What you think they need vs what they think they want

You are now working with your client. It might be individual work, or it might be group work. You know your stuff. You know what it is that people need in order to solve their problems, move to the next level, and achieve their goals. But—and here comes the million dollar question—do they know what they need? The chances are, to be honest, no they don't.

There's a great example of people not really understanding what it is that will work for them in Malcolm Gladwell's book Blink. He gets involved in a survey of speed-dating attendees. They have to fill in a form stating what it is they are looking for in their perfect partner, what it is they want for a great relationship. They then start the speed dating. At the end of it, they are questioned once again. This time they are asked which potential partners they liked and why.

Data was collated and reviewed. It was pointed out to the participants that what they said they wanted wasn't, in reality, what they had liked. So in preparation for the next week's session, they were given a list of what they had liked to guide them. Did they take any notice of it? No. They continued to seek out what it was they thought they wanted—regardless of what they had been told they liked.

There is a lesson in this for all of us. Just possibly, we as coaches and consultants have all the answers, but our clients may not take kindly to being told.

Much like in the strategy sessions, a large amount of the value we can bring is in helping our clients get to grips with what it is they really need versus what it is they want. Telling someone, as in the example above, what is better for them doesn't work. The job of the coach or consultant is to help the client understand for themselves why you have mapped out the journey the way you have and to help them create an emotional connection to it so that you weave together both what it is they need and what it is they want!

A few years back the double-glazing firm Everest put out an advertisement.

If I asked you to tell me what you wanted from having double-glazing installed, you'd likely talk about energy efficiency, soundproofing, and/or draught prevention. These are practical answers, but they're not likely to inspire others to go out and make a purchase. (I admit there are some of you who would be thrilled by those promises.)

The advert that they ran contained absolutely no information about the thickness of the glass or the brilliance of the fitting. What they talked about was the impact it would have on the lives of those who chose to fit it. They talked safety, warmth, family, and home. They spoke to human emotion, and it is the human emotion that will connect your client to the journey you are travelling together.

They want a promotion to feel proud. They want to build a business that creates financial stability (and therefore happiness for their family). They want to lose weight so that they can feel confident. For each step of the journey, you want to help them find that emotional connection. That way you will be able to give them what they need and they will get what they want.

And talking of journeys, let's take a look at what one of those might look like.

The client journey

As human beings we love the sense of journey. We like to know where we're going and how we are going to get there.

It's the same when we ask someone for help. The reason we ask for help is we are in a place where we are quite literally lost. We don't know what to do, or we have so many options we find it impossible to choose. We're in that overwhelming place like Alice in Wonderland—if we don't know where we're going, it doesn't matter which route we take, so we just stay fixed to the spot.

The transformation we want eludes us because of our inability to move forward.

Coaches in particular can really struggle with the paradox that is created by purist coaching teaching that says it is all about the client discovering their journey for themselves whilst the client is sitting there desperately needing some straightforward advice!

Simply put, we need to coach clients to reveal their destination, give them the steps to get there, and then coach them through what they will do at each step.

Coaching then becomes the mode to work with them to help them discover what works best for them, how they can play to their strengths, to reveal where they will need support to be successful, and so on. Telling someone, 'Let's see what happens', inspires neither comfort nor confidence. You want your client to be confident that you can help them. And why would you not share your expertise?

When it comes to consulting, it can often be the complete opposite. Clients expect you to know exactly what you should do to solve their challenges. It's almost like they think there's a magic wand you can wave and suddenly everything is alright, without any information gathering, interviewing, or diagnostics taking place. You have the opposite challenge here!

However, in both cases, being able to signpost the steps and support the steps with exercises, workshops, topic-specific coaching, etc. will help the client see that the destination can be reached, success is possible, and there are clear steps to take in order to get there.

That sense of being overwhelmed disappears, and they can move forward.

This is about you providing them with a blueprint to reach their destination, combining your expertise—you know the steps they should take—with your skills to help them find the best way to do it.

Let's make this real. Get a pen and paper. Mark up a timeline with seven stages, something like this:

Start	1	2	3	4	5	Finish

There are seven steps here. 'Start' is where your perfect, potential client is right now. It is where they are stuck, struggling, confused, needing help.

'Finish' is their destination, where they want to be.

You are about to design a coaching programme that you want to offer to your perfect, potential clients. Consider what the five steps are that they will need to take to move from 'Start' to 'Finish'. The likelihood is that their challenge is big enough to need five steps, but you can vary the number as you think appropriate. (Odd numbers always work well.)

Remember, you will cover some of these steps in the face-to-face time you have together; others might be covered in coaching sessions and/or homework.

Designing a coaching programme is fun, so use your knowledge and expertise. Start by brainstorming what the steps will be to get them to where they want to be, using the guidance below to help you.

To bring it to life, let me share an example of a client I coached and the five-step journey I designed for them. This was over a period of six months.

The client came to me wanting to make a career shift out of corporate and into consultancy. They were feeling stuck. They felt there was more out there to do, and they had dreams of a portfolio lifestyle—travelling the world whilot having time to indulge some of their hobbies whilst having a fulfilling career.

Start – Where the client is. Some of this will have been revealed in the strategy session, but you'll uncover more as you work together. This first step is about helping them understand what exactly is going on that is not working. Before the next step, send them your questionnaire or your diagnostic tool so that you can glean more information about them.

Step 1 – Defining the destination and mapping the journey. Step 1 is your first real time together, so doing a combination of big-picture work, which is very motivating, in addition to sharing the steps you will be taking together will get them in a great place to go and do some work on their own. This step helps them really connect with their goal and gives you the chance to find out more about what it is that makes them tick. Remember your diagnostic tool. Spend some time working through the results and drawing out what is going to be useful for them moving forward.

I spent Step 1 with my client getting clarity on the future—what that meant for them and their family. We talked finance as well as how they wanted to work and where (all the items in the foundations section). We talked about what it would feel like and the time frame within which they wanted to achieve this. We also worked through the implications of the results from their leadership-profiling tool and were able to understand which points of the journey would be easy and where they were likely to find it tough.

There is always a lot to do in the first step, which is why spending at least a half day if not a whole day works really well. Give your client some homework at the end—just a few simple tasks to take away (it will have been a full day)—and they will stay really engaged.

Step 2 – Taking action to create the dream. This is a time to review the client's progress and nail down the next essential items on the to-do list.

In the case of my client, we spent time at step 2 exploring opportunities for consultancy work. We looked at who their perfect, potential clients might be, nailed their expertise statement, and also identified some possible associate opportunities.

During the time you spend with your clients, it's important to actually achieve tasks and not just talk about them. It will remind clients just how quickly things can get done when they are focused.

Step 3 – Integrating the transformation into daily life. Step 3 is when you take it up a notch. Action must be happening by this step. If it isn't, it is really important to spend time finding out why not. There should be a significant shift going on at this point. They should be feeling excited as they have glimpsed what is possible from the action taken so far.

My client by this stage was really taking steps to make change. They had applied for and gotten a new job that was much closer to what they ultimately wanted to do. It gave them flexibility and provided the opportunity for more travel. They also had greater autonomy, so they were beginning to feel what it would be like to be a consultant, and they negotiated a pretty good package at the same time.

Step 4 – Exploring current opportunities. What opportunities are there right under your client's nose? Who is in their network? What simple shift could they make that would reap great rewards? Step 4 is a great place to do something creative to lift energy levels. It is here your client might be feeling the dip. Bring their dream clearly back to the centre of the work you are doing together.

At step 4 my client was feeling the dip. It had almost gone too smoothly! Therefore, it became time to reflect on what had been achieved so far and to appreciate the distance travelled. We spent time at this stage asking what would make this easy. We looked at current connections they had and set them up to have some exploratory conversations with those people. We slowed the pace a bit so that they could breathe.

Step 5 – Horizon scan. Now is the time to look forward and to increase the pace. Step 4 gave your client some breathing space; so Step 5 is the moment to create the next big action. Set one key task they must complete or achieve so that when you meet for the 'Finish', there is something to celebrate.

Part of my client's dream had been to move back home, and it was at step 5 that we discussed looking into whether this could happen and when. Moving home would be the time when they could seriously contemplate setting up their own portfolio business, so we knew this was both a physical and mental leap.

Finish – The destination. This is all about celebration. Now is the time to appreciate the tasks completed, to learn from what didn't go so well, and to spend some time planning the next phase. This is also your opportunity to talk about working together to support them through the next part of their journey.

Last year, this client moved back home. They have continued in their current consulting role, enjoying the travel, enjoying the freedom, and creating connections that will be invaluable to them when it comes time to start their own business. And as for that, we'll be working together next year to make that happen.

Remember, when a perfect, potential client appears in front of you, you can not only promise to help them reach their goal, but also help them see how they will get there—one step at a time.

Let's now move onto something practical. What might be some of the supporting materials you could use with your clients?

Tangibles

What do I mean by tangibles? I mean the materials you create (e.g., handouts, workbooks, quiz sheets, questionnaires, etc.) that people can work with, materials they can take away after spending time with you, materials they can refer back to from their desks or homes (which, very usefully, means you stay ever present in their minds).

Why would you create them? Because they are one of the best ways to have your client engage, remember, and take action well past the coaching or the workshop they had with you.

Keeping tangibles really simple is the biggest challenge when it comes to creating them. They should be designed to support the learning, the shift, or the transformation—not to add further content.

So you can breathe easy. I'm not suggesting you create a whole load more content. Tangibles are there to help the information sink in, to be able to apply the learning and make it personal. It's about making the journey with you real.

Adults have a pretty short attention span when it comes to taking in new information. I also believe (and this is particularly important when it comes to organisational work) that people don't engage unless there's something in it for them. If they have their own workbook, their own quiz sheet, etc., they'll want to engage.

Realising this was a big turning point for me, both

with individual clients and workshops—but particularly workshops because you can't give the amount of attention you would like to each individual. I NEVER deliver a workshop now without some handout(s) that participants can work on.

I never deliver a coaching VIP day without providing a workbook. Let me give you some examples of exactly what I mean by this. Last year I ran a workshop multiple times (designed and then repeated for a particular client—so, productised!).

The workshop was about how to be a high-performing team, so I started the workshop with a handout that was a tick-box exercise where each participant rated their team. They did this as individuals and then looked at it as a whole. The statements were based around research on the key elements of high-performing teams, so whilst they were ticking, they were also beginning to see and learn the differences between low and high performance.

I then gave them an additional handout that showed them five core 'must haves' for high performance. With that and a bunch of Post-its, they worked through an exercise brainstorming which of the five elements they needed to focus on first and what they would do.

Finally, I handed out my Top 10 tips for creating high performance—short, one-line suggestions of what they could do.

All of this was easy to produce. It helped the learning stick, and it gave them something to take away and continue to work with if they wished. All branded—

of course.

An example of another 'tangible' would be a deck of leadership cards I designed. I use them often with one-on-one clients. The cards have fifty-two different leadership behaviours, and I ask clients to pick out the behaviours they want to work on, the behaviours they think exemplify great leadership, or one of another dozen exercises you can do with them.

These cards are deceptively simple, but they make people's eyes light up. They get to join in, they get engaged, they even play! There, I'm giving all my secrets away!

Few clients want to start with a blank piece of paper, and activity adds a richness to the session that you just wouldn't get in a normal coaching conversation.

One warning point: Be careful. Avoid lots of separate handouts. It can start to get messy with loose sheets of paper and people losing track of which one they're working on.

If I'm doing a full day's workshop, or more than a day, I turn the handouts into a workbook with a nice cover on the front, single pages for each exercise, large fonts, and plenty of space for answers with lines. This way you give your clients a structure that makes it easy for them to see the steps they will take and to write down their own thoughts on how they are going to take those steps. As coaches, we all know the power is in our clients coming up with the how!

Before I finish this section, I want to cover one tangible in particular, and that's a profiling tool. By this I mean something that clients can use to rate themselves, whether that's by how often they do something, how important something is to them, what their preferences or strengths are about a particular topic, etc.

Yes, there are lots of really great profiling tools out there, particularly personality-based ones, and you want to use those as personality tools are complex to test and create for yourself. But for any other type of tool, you should consider creating your own—with one caveat. Always use them for individuals to rate themselves. If you want to create a profiler where others rate your client, you must be very, very careful that the questions have the same meaning for each person; otherwise, the data can be seriously distorted.

Tangibles are a low-cost way to engage clients. They are a great way to showcase the value you add, and they are simple to create. (Remember, it's not about more content; it's about exercises around the content already created.) All you need to do is keep the design simple, brand it so that people know how to find you if they need to, find a decent printer, and you're ready to go. And don't be cheap—print in colour!

What next?

I've touched on this before, but I just want to briefly remind you that you want to be prepared to have a great answer when your client asks you, 'What next?'

Do you just say good luck and goodbye, or do you offer them the chance to continue to work with you? And if you do make that offer, what is it you are offering? The same, something more, something less, or something different?

Keep in mind a change of pace and tempo can be energising.

When your client asks, 'What next?' what will you say?

Your options are many, but your client will be looking for you to be their guide, so just be ready to offer either the next level up or possibly a more self-sufficient one level down, if they want to work more under their own steam for a while.

Consider three different ways, at different levels and at different price points, that clients can work with you.

As you start to shape the 'what next', keep in mind your preferences, how you work best, and what energises you so that when you're in front of clients, you are energising them!

ENGAGE

'Since you cannot do good to all, you are to pay special attention to those who, by the accidents of time, or place, or circumstances, are bought into closer connection with you.'

– Saint Augustine

In this next section I want to cover ways to stay connected and engaged with your clients and perfect, potential clients so that you can reduce the amount of your time you are spending on sales activities (non-billable time) and therefore have more time to work with clients.

I'm going to share with you how to make sure your clients are aware of what else it is you do, how to stay on their radar, and how you will know which clients are the best ones for you to focus this activity on. I want to start with sowing seeds.

Sowing seeds

This has to be one of my favourite marketing activities. Done well, it is a simple, elegant way to market yourself. And it's a key tool for both repeat business and referral business.

So what do I mean by seeding? 'Seeding' is a marketing term. It's about planting 'seeds' in your conversations with your clients or your perfect, potential clients about how you work and what you have achieved when working with others. Think of it like literally scattering seeds that tell them about who you are and what you do and, as I can't emphasise it enough, the change and transformation you have brought about.

This isn't about waiting for someone to ask the obligatory 'So what do you do?' question. This is about thinking ahead about which stories you want to share—which are the ones in which you shine most brightly. So you want to prepare your seeds in advance. Have some for those in-the-moment opportunities, some that reflect your core expertise and strengths, and others that are specific to a topic you are sharing with a group or an individual.

Not seeding strategically is probably the biggest missed opportunity I see when watching consultants and coaches in action. There are always chances to seed; it's a case of making it relevant and not overdoing it!

Why do it?

When you were reading the 'Your offer' section, were you griping when I suggested you not tell everyone everything you do in the very first meeting? If so, I hope seeding offers you a good reason to follow my suggestion and a good way to drip feed your expertise instead of creating an overwhelming and confusing flood!

I have a bit of a reputation of being fantastic at creating repeat business. I'm not bragging. As far as I was concerned, for many years, it just happened! It took a little while to spot why, but a few years back I was able to pinpoint that I naturally use seeding, partly because I like to share stories to motivate others, and partly because I also like to help people see the next possible steps.

Let's take a look at what this looks like in reality.

When I first started out and I would win a piece of work or be hired as a coach, I would scope what we were going to work on, what tools we needed for the job, and what actions had to be taken—all good stuff. When the time came to complete the work, there were lots of thank you's and then goodbye, and I'd be on to the next client.

Now, here's the thing. They probably hired me to work on something pretty specific, which is great. I got to show my expertise in that area. But what if they could have benefited from other things I'm really good at? I needed them to know about those other 'things', but waiting until the final session (or even worse, after the final session) to start talking about what else we could do felt really clunky.

So what's the alternative?

The alternative is to sow seeds throughout the relationship. Your intention is to inform, not to sell!

Let me share with you here three ways you can seed that will create opportunities to continue to work with your client after the end of what we will now see as the first phase.

1. Share what you are up to

Let your client know what other topics you are working on at that time with other clients. This helps her/him understand the breadth of what you do, and human curiosity ensures they will be interested! If a client asks me how I am, I will often say something like, 'I'm good. I've been really busy working on a great project with someone that involves ....' I'll be sure that what I'm sharing is relevant and something I know they might be interested in. If I'm working with a team, I will weave in how I've helped others with the problems they are tackling or the goals they want to reach, being careful to talk about the outcome.

2. Be ready to talk about your successes

When clients mention a problem they are having, share how you have worked on that exact same thing and resolved it for someone else. Remember to share the impact you had and be careful not to talk using the 'royal we'! I hear 'we' used a lot when you should be saying 'I'. If someone asks what you're currently working on with a client and you say, 'We've just had a major breakthrough, and they got their promotion', that's not very powerful. Instead, why not say, 'I suggested a process for a client that successfully got them the promotion they've been after for ages'. Claim your success!

3. Offer a current client a taster session

Consider doing what I did last week: offer your client a taster session in an area in which you're not working with them yet so that they can see the value and appreciate the gift. I offered a workshop for twelve people (in an organisation with 150 managers). For me, it's both about appreciation and investment. N.B. This is for current clients who have spent money with me, not for prospective ones.

So even if you're just starting out and you have just a couple new clients, think about stories you can share so that they can see what else you can offer in the next step of your journey together.

If you don't do this, this is what happens. (It's happened to me, and I know countless others who've recounted something similar.)

A client has hired you to facilitate a four-hour session with their senior management team to look at where the company is going next and what they need to focus on. This is going to be a session about strategy and leadership as well as getting them into that visioning space. You go along, do a great job, leave at the end, and everyone says thanks, that was great.

After the session they have a discussion amongst themselves, and they come up with the idea that they should all get some one-on-one coaching around the topic. They go off, talk to HR, and get introduced to some coaches. But guess what—you're not one of them because they didn't know you did that sort of work, so they didn't think to mention it to you!

So what would you do differently? How do you let them know what you do without sounding like a cheesy salesperson who's a jack-of-all-trades?

In the example above you would have said something like, 'A couple months back I was coaching a senior manager on this exact challenge. She was up against (state the problem). I worked with her to (state what you did) and then (share what happened—the outcome).' Obviously, you are all the while respecting any confidentiality!

I honestly can't remember the last time I didn't get repeat work with a client. Seeding takes the pressure off worrying that they won't get how broad your skillset/knowledge bank is. You're going to be able to share that with them as you work with them. Seeding also means that you can work with a client step-by-step on a journey, and they won't have to sign up for the whole shebang in one go.

Creating repeat business with clients you love takes a little skill and patience, but the dividends are huge, including more stability in income, less cold selling, and the opportunity to develop a relationship that allows you to flex your expertise and skillset whilst staying in a place of value and integrity. Oh, and don't forget the joy of less selling and more working—think of the profit ratio!

4. Connect

You've probably realised that at this stage in the book it's now all about how to make the most of the client relationships that you are creating.

As you grow your business, there is a lot to learn—and a lot to do! Taking it step-by-step means you have the time to transition through the challenge of new ways of working and, with familiarisation and success, turn them into habits, which then frees up time to learn more new ways of working!

You are able to add layers and richness to your business whilst avoiding feeling overwhelmed and frustrated. Trying to do everything all at the same time is what makes setting up a business so exhausting, and to be honest, you start to hate what you thought you loved. That is not good.

All of this brings us now to enhancing your client connections.

Much like sowing seeds, nurturing connections with clients is the way to get repeat business.

What are some of the rules about what creates great connections?

- It must be personal.
- It must add value.
- It must be relevant.
- It isn't about selling.
- It is about informing.

I want to talk a bit about why I use these five rules to check in with how I'm staying connected with clients, and then I'll talk a bit about how to manage this and easy ways to do it. Let me remind you though, I'm not talking about the need to stay in touch with thousands of people. (I'll cover social media in the next section.)

Here and now I want you to think about your current clients. (You can also apply this to your perfect, potential clients, but I'm only talking about those who are *a perfect fit*. This way of connecting is for small numbers, not every possible random, maybe, 'might happen' client.)

The way you connect will vary, and wherever possible, do use the phone! Human contact is a rare commodity these days, and if you're calling them to share something that fits the above five rules, I promise you they will be delighted to hear from you.

This is really all about customer relationship management, or CRM as it's known in the marketing world. But to be honest, whenever I hear someone say 'CRM', I think of some huge data file somewhere with thousands of pieces of information on it that no one ever actually does much with! Apologies if CRM is your thing!

One of the best mindset approaches, and one that is super appreciated by clients, is to see yourself as a curator of information. Don't get yourself into a spin that everything you share has to be written or designed by you for it to be worthy. You can add value by sending someone a link to an article that highlights a recent problem they were talking to you about and offers a solution to it, or by pointing out to them a conference next month with a speaker that you know they would love to see.

You also become known as a font of knowledge and interesting 'things', which means they will start picking up the phone to connect with you!

So where do you start?

I'd love you to work through this right now so that you can see it's not a huge task.

Think of one of your clients. (You can do this for all your clients, but let's take one to make it real.)

- Client name?
- What are you currently working on with them?
- What is currently really resonating or motivating them to take action? This might be something you have done with them, or just a way that you've discovered works.
- What might be a related topic of interest (that might also be a seeding opportunity for you)?
- What do they like doing outside work?

Here's an example of what this looks like:

Client?

Patricia

What am I currently working on with her?

Getting her business into profit through getting more clients

What is currently really resonating or motivating her to take action?

Seeing herself as financially independent

What might be a related topic of interest (for sending articles, information, etc.)?

Personal branding

What does she like doing outside work?

She's an art exhibition junky.

Can you see how quickly you can find or keep an eye out for something that would interest her? And you don't have to spend ages looking for personal, valuable, relevant, useful information.

For example, I can send her tips and information on getting clients. I can forward her news snippets and articles about personal branding. If I spot something interesting art-wise in the weekend papers, I can let her know.

Don't overdo it. Just the occasional 'I was thinking of you' note will help you both stay connected to each other. Think of it as small, helpful gifts.

So how can you find this type of information if nothing has popped out at you recently? If you want to actively source information that you know your clients will love, then clearly the Internet is the place to go.

Now, I'm not some sort of techy whizz. I'm a leadership development consultant and coach who likes using the Internet to make life easy. So for sourcing information that clients will love, I want to share a couple tools that help me do this, to make it easy for you.

Software for me—to quote William Morris—has to be either beautiful or useful, or both! And so much out there isn't!

For sourcing information, I keep an eye out for good blogs. Good blogs often lead you to great articles. I'm pretty strict on how many I follow—they have to be really good.

If there's a particular subject you want to keep an eye on, try searching for 'Top 10 (insert your topic) blogs', or 'best blogs for (insert topic)'. Be ruthless. Follow the ones you really like and ditch the ones you don't.

My favourite online tool for following blogs is bloglovin (www.bloglovin.com). It passes both the beautiful and useful test. Simply set up an account—it's free—and you can then search for, or paste in the URLs of, blogs you want to follow.

Keep in mind, you're likely sourcing information for no more than twelve to fifteen people. The focus for this is on your current clients and/or a couple perfect, potential clients.

I'm on the move quite a bit, so if I do see something of interest, it's not always the right time to zap it off to someone, but I don't want to forget to do it, and I don't want to lose it. To avoid this, I use Microsoft OneNote. I have a separate tab for each client, and I just paste whatever bit of information I want on the right tab for the right client.

There are lots of other ways to do this, and you probably have some favourites, so do what works for you. Just make sure it's mobile and easy!

This makes connecting pretty effortless. You stay on your clients' radar, and they get great short, useful updates from you. Everyone wins.

Virtual presence

Up until now I've intentionally avoided talking about your virtual presence, by which I mean, for the sake of this chapter, your website and the use of social media. There are a couple good reasons for that.

Both can be amazingly time-consuming and great distractions, distractions that take you away from your most important task, which is to get in front of your perfect, potential clients—in person.

I also see a lot of people struggle with their virtual presence because they haven't worked out the foundations of their business and therefore aren't quite sure either how to position themselves or how to create content that will captivate their audience. This means as you build a website and create content for social sharing, it can feel like really hard work.

Finally, to become good at copywriting takes some practice. It's not a natural strength for most people, and it's not something I profess to be brilliant at, but with practice I have certainly gotten better.

I also want to be really clear here and say that I'm not a social media or web expert. As you well know, there are plenty out there. What I am, though, is someone who runs a business and keeps a virtual presence up and running, so I want to use this section to give you a few tips and hints on how to approach being present without allowing it to take up enormous amounts of your time—time you could be connecting with people in person (always the best method of marketing).

This topic could take over the whole book, so excuse me for keeping it brief. It being brief, though, is a reminder not to let it take over your whole life!

Let's start with a website. Do you need one?

Yes, you do, and I want to talk about the essential pages you need to have up when you first get started. Your site doesn't have to be all singing, all dancing on day one. (That can overwhelm both you and your visitors.) What it does need to do is reflect you and what your business is about—really clearly.

When someone arrives at your site, they should immediately understand what it is you do. (A good tag line is enormously helpful with this.)

Once they have grasped that, all your pages should reinforce that. So let's look at which pages you want there. On the front page you want to offer a gift. You also want a well-written 'about' page, an invitation to 'work with me' page, and a way for people to get in contact with you.

The gift:

These days, the offer of a gift in return for an e-mail address is so common that the pressure is on to provide a really great gift that people can't resist. This gift needs to be all about solving the biggest pain your potential, perfect clients are feeling. You also want it to showcase just how good you are, so make sure it is really useful and really neat and tidy—it doesn't need lots of design work (unless you're a designer or someone providing a visual service).

The about page:

Everything on your site should talk about your perfect, potential client and talk to their struggles and dreams—even your about page! The standard logic is that this is the page where you talk all about **you**. However, you don't want to do that. This a great page to talk about how you and your experience, strengths, skills, etc. can transform the lives of others. So position the content in a 'this is how I can help you' way.

Work with me:

From the previous chapters, you are now clear about how you want to work with clients and the journey you will offer them. Draw on that work to create your 'work with me' page.

As a minimum, you want to offer a strategy/discovery session, and sometimes just having this can work fantastically as the visitor is faced with a simple choice—sign up or move on.

Testimonials:

This is probably the second-most popular page on my site. I see that people go from the front page, to the about page, and then to testimonials. They are definitely checking me out!

You might panic at this page, concerned that you don't have any testimonials yet. Here are some ideas of where to find some, or how to generate some quickly.

- At the end of any strategy/discovery session that you do, if it's gone well, ask for a testimonial. You want to ask them what has changed for them through having the discussion so that you capture transformation.
- If you've just stepped out of being employed, look back to comments made on your performance reviews or to any 360 development in which you participated. There can be some really great comments in there.
- Call up a few people you used to work with and ask them if they would give you a testimonial.

For all of these, make sure they are talking about what it is you are doing now.

The contact page:

The final page for your new website is a 'contact' page. Create a simple form for this so that if people want to ask a question or get in touch with you, they can do so easily. Don't put your e-mail address anywhere on this page or anywhere on your site—you will be inundated with spam!

When you start out, think of a website as support for what you do rather than as a big part of how to get clients. It needs to be a really useful place where people can check you out and get some more information about you.

For example, if I've been out speaking to a group, the next day the number of people visiting my site climbs. No surprises there. And often, when I talk to someone who has been referred to me, the first thing they say is that they've taken a look at my site. It becomes a wonderful reinforcement, confirming to perfect, potential clients that you're someone worth speaking to and hopefully working with.

As you grow your business, your website will become much more important, but for now, keep it looking good, keep it on message, and keep it consistent in both style and content. Useful and beautiful!

Now, on to social media!

Oh boy! For someone just starting out, this has to be the biggest time sucker out there, so here are a few rules on how to engage with it.

- Start with just one social media channel, be that Facebook, Twitter, LinkedIn, etc. Choose one where your perfect, potential clients are hanging out. That is the reason you are using it. Choose a channel that you like, and get used to using it before you add another.
- Set a time limit each week as to how much time you spend on it. Focus one-third of that time on engaging and responding to others and two-thirds to posting yourself.
- Create a list of possible things to post. Once I did this, social media posting became a whole lot easier. Some ideas are quotes, articles, interesting facts and statistics, links back to your site (but not too often), a book recommend, or a sentence to complete. Vary them as you go and you will never be without content.
- Plan what you are going to post. Planning prevents you from going online and getting

distracted. Remember, you can post interesting snippets other people's articles. What you are doing with your posts is showing people you are a font of knowledge—the person to go to who knows what is going on out there! Depending on which channel you use, you might be posting once a day or fifteen times a day!

- Using software means you can put all your posts up in one go and then let it send them out across the week. My favourite for this is bufferapp.com, but there are others out there that I'm sure are equally good.

Tracking

Your business is up and running! Congratulations! When you look at the statistics for how many start-ups fail in the first year, recognise what you have achieved. It's a proper business now.

You know who you are and what it is you do. You have a roster of clients, your revenue streams are set up, some perfect potentials are in the pipeline, and it's feeling real.

Now is the time to put some simple behind-the-scenes mechanics in place so that you have tangible proof of the success you are creating.

It's time to start tracking what you do, analysing what's working and what isn't, and enjoying the excitement of projections turning into reality.

You may be someone who has tracked your business since the beginning. If you are, well done! You're in the minority! Too often I see coaches and consultants not tracking at all. This may be because they're afraid of what they might find out, it may be because the numbers aren't exciting, it may even be that's just how they do things. However, if you want to grow your business and you want to make it easy to do so, tracking gives you a heap of really useful information to help with your decision making as you move forward.

I know … it can sound really boring. But before you switch off or start yawning, keep this in mind: In my experience of working with non-trackers (as I like to call them), they get very frustrated (and so do I!) because they don't know what's worked really well. They don't know who their best clients are, and guessing at this type of information is dangerous. They don't know which investments have paid off—did they learn something that they've put into action? Did they get more clients? Finally, and this is probably the best reason of all, tracking what you've achieved can be one of the quickest confidence boosters around. There's something of the pessimist in all of us, and tracking can often show us that our pessimism is misplaced.

So what should you be tracking? I could get geeky about this, but there are some obvious fundamentals here if you want your business to flourish.

Time – What you are doing with the time you have allocated as work time? And how is what you are doing positively impacting your bottom line? This helps establish where time is being frittered and where it's being put to good use. Not everything has to make money, but it has to be a means to potentially making money! And talking of money …

Money coming in – What targets are you setting for yourself for each month and each year? Are you reaching or exceeding those targets? (You will get what you wish for!)

Money going out – Here I'm talking specifically about your business outgoings. There are two investments that I won't ever give up: investing in myself (I allow a minimum of 10 percent of my revenue to be spent on learning) and investing in having the right kit to do the job—laptops, phones, software, etc. Don't make life difficult by being stingy.

Client/revenue ratio – Which clients are you working with, and what is the revenue generated with each one? If you have several different income streams, track each one individually. To help you do this, you can download my Income Stream Calculator here www.getclients101.com/toolkit. I've used a version of this since day one with my business, and it's been invaluable both to project income and to track it coming in.

Let me share a couple examples of why this is a good thing to do.

A couple years back I was working with someone who was coaching in the entrepreneur niche. She's really smart, knows her stuff, used to find it really easy to get in the press, and had clients, but she clearly wasn't satisfied with where she was.

The most amusing thing was when I asked her where she was, there was no way to quantify it. Yes, she knew her previous year's income from submitting her figures for tax. Did she know what she'd earned this year? No. Did she know which clients were working out best for her? No. Was work feeling better or worse? Worse. And yet, when we spent some time on the figures and looked at her client list, she was actually doing almost twice as well as the previous year.

It didn't take long to get her back into a place of confidence and moving forward! It also helped her make some decisions about which clients she wanted to work with in the future.

Sometimes we have to turn to the hard facts to get a

true picture of reality.

And I'll confess, just recently I realised I had stopped tracking my coaching hours. (Some coaching associations ask for evidence of this, and I'd recently decided there is one I want to join.)

I needed to evidence a minimum of 200 hours of coaching. For love or money, I couldn't come up with an educated guess of how many hours I'd done over the last year or so.

Thanks to an electronic diary, I was able to go back over the last two years and tot up the hours. I easily got within the minimum, and the data I pulled together, though I originally did it just to find out how many hours I had been spent coaching, also served me in other ways.

Simply and psychologically, it reminded me that I had done a lot of coaching. That felt good. When you mix consulting and coaching together, it can sometimes just all get a bit lost.

There was a whole list of clients with whom I haven't been in touch for a while. (Note to self: connect, connect, connect!)

I hadn't realised the different ways I coach—individuals, teams, programmes, random one-off sessions. I was able to look at which ones had worked best and with whom, and then I was able to work out why. Now I know the ideal way forward for me and my clients.

And all I'd done was spend an hour pulling the data

together.

None of this is difficult to do if you decide you're going to do it. Put a couple hours aside each month and track your time, your money in and out, and your revenue by specific client. That data will be your future gold.

DO DIFFERENT – SMARTLY

'The real voyage of discovery consists not in seeking new landscapes, but in having new eyes.'

– Marcel Proust

Repurpose

When I'm working with clients to develop their leadership capabilities, the first thing I say to them is that it's not about doing more; it's about doing things differently.

That can cause quite a bit of consternation, and the word 'but' appears frequently as they justify their belief that there is nothing they can give up; that if they want to achieve more, they have to do more; that only they can be the ones to pull off the task—no one else quite gets it.

As a confessed control freak, all I can say is I'm so delighted that I no longer think like this. It comes as a huge relief to develop trust in others (there are people out there who can actually make a better job of it than I can), and to be able to focus my time on what I'm good at instead of fiddling around with web pages wondering why those bullet points just won't go where I want. (Oh, yes, I can confess to days spent doing that sort of thing.)

For you to take the next step in your business, it's time to do things differently. And that's what this whole section—Do differently - smartly—is about. I'm going to cover repurposing, working with clients virtually, and ways to build a team around you.

These are three key things I have been working through over the last two years. By doing these three things, I was able to come out of recession and have a six-figure year (sterling, not dollars). And though I wouldn't wish recession on anyone, it gave me time to reflect, plan, and take action—to do things differently.

Let's talk repurposing.

Repurposing is about taking something you have created—that might be a programme, a workshop, or a system that you use—and offering it to clients in many different formats. When I first looked at doing this, I wasn't sure if I was comfortable. I questioned the value of selling the same thing, in a different. The point I completely missed is that my clients want the same thing in different formats because it gives them a choice. That choice may be based on price, it may be based on the time they have available to learn something new, or it may be based on the method with which they prefer to work.

This meant that what I had been doing in the past, offering a learning experience in a single format, actually wasn't helpful at all.

Repurposing also means that you can create and design in a cost-effective way and pass that cost efficiency on to your clients. Or it may mean that when they pay you for design, that time gets spent on refining and tailoring it so that it's spot on for them.

Here's an example of what I'm talking about from the world of retail. I was recently out shopping and decided to treat myself to some perfume.

This type of product is a perfect example of taking one item (in this case, perfume) and packaging it in many different ways, for different uses and different purposes.

I'd decided I wanted some Elie Saab perfume, having been swayed by a free sampler in a magazine (their version of a strategy session!). As I stood in the store, here were my choices: two sizes of eau de parfum, three sizes of eau de toilette, shower gel, and soap. Basically, it was the same product packaged in many different ways to meet different pockets. Think about it. You can do exactly the same thing, and you will be giving your client a choice—not too much choice to confuse them—but enough to purchase what you do in a way that works for them.

At this stage in your business, you will have designed quite a few different interventions. You may already have repurposed some of that design, but let's take a look at some ways you could be repurposing what you do. By the way, this book came about from repurposing a webinar I did on seven steps to a client-getting mindset!

Let's take a workshop you ran recently. It lasted a day. The participants loved it, so you know the content was good. It involved a PowerPoint presentation and maybe a participant workbook or at least some handouts. Instead of just filing it away, start to think about how you could take that content and turn it into something different and really useful for this client or new ones. Here are some ideas:

- Record a downloadable follow-up for that client, incorporating the slides with a voice-over for a small additional fee.

- Create an e-book from the content that you can offer to other clients who might want to get a taste of what you do at low cost.

- Create three mini two-hour workshops by breaking the content down and then framing it into learning bites.

- Create a six-step coaching programme targeting clients who are seeking to work through this particular issue.

The list goes on. You know your content, so go and dig something out and play around with repurposing it. When you have a good idea and a skeleton design, let those clients with whom you're staying connected know all about it and see how they respond.

Repurposing is all about you making the most of your time and providing your clients with quality, accessible learning in a way that works for them. It is also a brilliant way to grow your business from the core of what you love doing. There's a whole new selection of revenue streams for you to discover. Part of this discovery is making use of the virtual facilities now available to us, so that's what we're going to cover next.

Virtual delivery

There is no getting away from the fact that integrating online learning into your work is critical if your business is to thrive in the future (and the only way this doesn't apply to you is if you're just about to retire!).

Why? Because the majority of your client base is going to expect you to be online in one form or other, and you will start to stand out for all the wrong reasons—as old-fashioned and of another generation, as just not 'getting' what people want. You must make use of the virtual space and facilities on offer. And it can be fun!

As a coach or consultant, you're in the field of learning. You are more than likely working with busy adults, possibly cash-rich and definitely time-poor adults.

E-learning is a $56.2 billion industry, and by the end of 2015, that figure will have doubled (elearningindustry.com).

The most recent generation joining the workforce are considered digital natives—people for whom the Internet is an integral part of their lives. They couldn't and won't live without it. They will have also experienced online learning throughout their education, so for them, it really is normal.

You may be very keen to embrace virtual delivery as part of what you do. Good! It will feel easier with this mindset. On the other hand, you might be feeling nervous and concerned that it's just too much to take in and you don't know where to start.

The reason I have intentionally put this section towards the end of the book is that this topic is easier to absorb once you're clear on what your business is and what it is you do, as well as after you've been working in person with clients so that you know what works and what doesn't. The virtual world isn't that different.

Whether using technology appeals to you or not, I would strongly recommend you don't start spending vast amounts of your time learning all the ins and outs of setting up virtual delivery. You need to focus on getting clients and let others help you set up this newer element of your business. (It is the reason that building a team comes next.)

So what is virtual delivery? Here are some examples:

- Using the Internet to deliver a workshop live instead of being in a room
- Setting up learning modules on a web page that clients can access when they want
- Providing a forum space to allow clients to interact with each other, a place to congregate and share information that isn't easy to do in person
- Having a place for your coaching clients to go to access information to support their journey, where you can post articles and they can log progress or ask questions
- Providing follow-up downloads for clients to reinforce face-to-face learning
- Running a webinar for which individuals can sign up and participate in

In the small-business world, the use of online delivery is very common, and when set up well, it can create a whole revenue stream of its own.

Remember, it's all about ease, accessibility, and reinforcing the learning. We are in a world where people want to learn at their own pace, to be able to listen on their iPods or in the car, or to take an hour out at a weekend.

You become very accessible without having to be accessible!

And whatever it is you want to do, I'm sure there is the technology to support it.

Let me share with you a couple ways I've used the Internet to successfully deliver work to clients over the last year.

For a recent train-the-trainer design for a global leadership development programme, I included bite-size recordings of the major parts of each workshop. These were simply visual and audio recordings explaining how to run each session, plus some hints and tips to make running it easier. This meant if they forgot what they were supposed to do (even if it was on the day of the workshop), they could quickly access the recordings and get a five-minute refresh—easy.

For coaching clients, I offer them the opportunity to have our coaching calls recorded, and then I can send them the file so that they can listen back over it at their leisure. For those on a specific programme, they have 24/7 access to all the materials we use throughout the programme, plus somewhere to keep a log of their progress.

Over the last six months I have designed and delivered a live virtual leadership development programme that has been broadcast across various countries in Africa. Though there were some technical challenges, it meant that leadership development could be delivered to a group of people for whom the cost of global travel had previously prevented them from taking part in this type of programme. We were able to share content, interact live, post comments, write on whiteboards, etc. It was exciting and fulfilling. The possibility that this could be done with clients scattered all over the world while I sat in my home office was truly brilliant.

Your virtual team

By now, you should be exploring lots of ways to do things differently, whether that is in repurposing your content, the materials you use, the workshops you run, or whether that's stepping further into the opportunities the web has to offer. One task that you want to keep focused on, however, is building your client list, and to be able to do that really well, you need to build the team around you.

We are so immensely fortunate to live in an era where having a virtual team with no single, fixed abode no longer fazes clients. I remember when I started out, clients often asked where my office was, or how many people I had working for me—it sounds positively prehistoric! Nowadays, clients are more likely to ask how I work with a team that is scattered and what tips can I give them!

This book focuses on how to build a great business as a one woman/man setup, so I'm not going to get into setting up an associate model where you have a team of consultants and coaches working for you. If that appeals to you, just remember that you will be doing a lot less delivery and a lot more leading of your business. That is a tough transition and a topic for another book!

Let's focus on you and the opportunity you have to grow your business without adding employees to a payroll. I'm not against employing others, but when you're starting to grow, that feels like a big step and there's an easier one available to you.

There are three things you need to do.

First, you need to start noting down—yes, literally writing down—each day the tasks that you've done, and you need to plot these tasks under two headings: 'tasks that had to be done by me' and 'tasks that could have been done by someone else'—who would have done it brilliantly. (There is a gremlin in all of us that says that others won't do it properly or as well as we would. For this exercise, you want to assume that anything being done by someone else is going to be done really well. That creates freedom for you instantly.)

The chances are you have a pretty eclectic mix of tasks—particularly, I hope, in the second column! If there's very little in that second column, give me a call. We need to talk!

Plot your tasks for two weeks. I suggest two weeks in the hope that during that time you've done a majority of what you do regularly and because after four to five days, you tend to start to let go of some of the tasks that you thought it essential that you do.

This is always a really great discussion stage with clients as they begin to see just how much they could let go of, and they start to wonder what they will do with the time that is freed up. (Who knows? They might write a book!) For some, it's easy to see what will fill that time—more getting-client activities. For others, the vacuum can seem daunting, and the desire to hold onto the known instead of venturing into the unknown can be paralysing.

It's impossible to create a step change if you don't know where it is you are stepping to next—and if that future place doesn't look exciting.

So for speed and to create action, scan over that list of tasks you could pass over to someone and have a rough guess of how many hours a week that would create for you. Can you see how doing things differently rather than doing more things works?

Let's say it frees up five hours of your time. Take a look at your 'tasks that have to be done by me' list. I'll give you a last chance to move any of those for which that statement isn't true and then look at which of those tasks you want to do more often. To give you some guidance, you want to do more of whatever will increase what you are doing with clients or what will get you more new clients.

So you're now thinking, 'That's all very well, Jo, but what about all those other tasks? I'm going to have to earn a fortune if I have to pay someone else to do them'. I have a few answers to that one.

First, it doesn't cost a fortune to have someone (or a group of people) run the back-office operations for you.

Second, the point of this is to increase your revenue. You must track that you are increasing revenue above the cost of paying someone to do the work.

Third, this is more about mindset than anything else. This is about trusting complete strangers (at first) to work on your business, which I know is precious to you. And you have to take that leap of faith; otherwise, you will stall.

I hope that you are already outsourcing your bookkeeping, tax returns, etc. If you're not, get that sorted now! You probably already outsource some of your web maintenance, or at least the more technical side of things.

That is where I was a few years back. And to be honest, I was getting a bit fed up of it. I had no time to experiment. If I wasn't working, I was doing admin, and the getting out and meeting people was suffering. I was truly fearful that my whole mojo was disappearing down a drain somewhere.

That's when I sat down and scoped out the lists above. I asked myself the big questions: What would I do in my business if I had more time? What would be fun? Which clients would I like to have? Where would I go to find them? It was easy to refill the diary with far more fruitful activities.

Now, here's what I did that I don't want you to do. I dipped my toe into the world of virtual assistance and signed up to work with an independent VA. It worked fine, but if I'd looked at my list properly, and if she had been a bit more honest about her skillset, we would have realised it was going to be a struggle. So I then worked with another VA. This time was better, but I realised I was asking for things that, to be fair to her, just weren't within her remit. So it was still feeling clunky, and it was supporting all my gremlin's whispers of 'you should just do it yourself'.

The turning point was when I made the decision to get serious about growing my business and started to search out VA support that offered a team. And this was where another mindset shift occurred. I had to use them a minimum of ten hours a month for them to take me on. Wow, that meant I had to create ten hours of work for them to do. Fortunately, they offer a huge range of different skills, so within a matter of weeks, and with a backlog of task wishes, I'd used up my ten hours and more.

I have a project manager assigned to me who spreads out the tasks based on the skills needed. As a team, they are hugely flexible and efficient, and what has been achieved over the last year has been amazing.

It's like getting a cleaner for the first time—you wonder how you ever did without them.

How did I go about tracking them down? I asked for recommendations and spread my net wide to anyone I could think of who might use this type of service. The team I work with is based in the U.S., and the time difference actually works really well for me as I can work in the morning and send tasks over for them to pick up when they wake up. More often than not, when I get up the following morning, it's all been done!

And, all joking aside, I would not have written this book if I hadn't been able to delegate work. I would not be able to juggle the various client assignments and relationships I have.

Yes, there are still tasks I hold onto, but I also know there are some that I will be letting go of—soon.

OPPORTUNITY

'If a window of opportunity appears, don't pull down the shade.'

– Tom Peters

Horizon scanning

Your business is successful, stable, and even predictable! You're happy and fulfilled, so what next? Is there a 'what next'?

Yes, there is because we live in a constantly shifting world where clients ebb and flow, where new information and learning are constantly revealed to us, and being pragmatic, because we're likely to get bored doing the same thing day in and day out. Coaches and consultants are natural explorers. It's time to lift your eyes from the desk and look out.

You have a team you can trust to support your business. You have tried and tested means of creating a business platform that is both high profit and high integrity. All of this means you are at a place where you have the chance to breathe in, look up, and see what is going on in the world, what opportunities are out there waiting for you.

Horizon scanning is all about possibilities, discovering new ways of working, identifying new people to work with. It's also about thinking ahead farther than twelve months' time; it's about creating the five- or ten-year plan.

Sure, life happens, and there will be events that will take you off course, slow you down, or even make you change direction, but don't wait for those events to dictate what you do. You will end up like a cork bobbing on the ocean—constantly being pushed and pulled to places you don't want to go. Choose your direction and then start walking.

There are a ton of complex ways that you can choose to do this, and there will be people insisting you need a 100-page business plan, documentation that nails in detail what you will do at every step, and a raft of other supporting activities that have a tendency to suck the life out of you. Yes, when you get closer to implementation, you need to test your choices. You need to do your research to be confident that your decisions are the right ones. But before that, you must find your motivation because, as you well know, when the going gets tough, you need something wonderful to hold on to.

When you look out across the horizon, what is it you're looking for? Remember, this is the long term. You won't achieve this tomorrow or the next day, so don't worry about what it is you have to do to get there right now. In fact, you probably won't know what it is. Just get that destination crystal clear in your mind so that you feel the adrenalin of a new challenge, your spirits lift, and your heart starts beating a little faster!

Here's what you need to do.

Let's make this simple.

Your first step is to pick a time frame. Is this your horizon in three years' time, five years' time, or ten years' time? Pick a time from now that works for you.

You might find it more useful to think about it from the perspective of how old you will be. I find that asking myself what I want to be doing at fifty, sixty, or seventy years old makes it pretty real!

Your next step is to work through the four W's—who, what, where, and when, and for each of these W's, there is one more. For each of these you want to also ask yourself why.

You can download a template to help you plot the answers to all of these at getclients101.com/toolkit.

When you come to answer all of these questions, you want to look back and learn from the past. Explore what worked REALLY well, and don't dwell on what didn't. Look forward to what it is you REALLY want.

Who?

The *who* is obvious. With which clients would you love to be working? Is it similar to your current clients, or is it a completely different client group? Is it about the people or the industry they work in? Would you love to work with scientists or celebrity chefs? Those who make money or those who help others? Who will have you leaping out of bed in the morning because you know you have a great day ahead. And why?

What?

By now you will have exposed yourself to a lot of different topics, so your expertise will be broader and stronger. Do you want to create more breadth in what you do and keep expanding that breadth, or do you want to start to specialise and get narrow and deep? And why?

Where?

This is such a great question and one of the areas I most love working through with clients because there is so much fun in it. It sparks all sorts of interesting and wild thoughts. This is the question that is so often avoided because coaches and consultants feel they don't have much choice in this matter. You have way more than you realise! The world is your oyster—dream on!

Practically, where do you want to be when you're working? Literally, do you like being out with clients? If so, where? Do you get a buzz from being in big cities, or do you love the idea of one-on-one or small group sessions in luxury hotels? Does 'international' ring bells for you? Is there a country in which you would love to spend more time? Could you live there half a year, delivering what you do now, but over there? Where is it you want to be when working? And why?

When?

Answering this question is like coming full circle from when you started out. When will you be working?

With a great team in place and lots of clients wanting to work with you, you are now in a position to say when you work and when you don't. Remember, this doesn't mean you're not still visible; you just set everything up to run smoothly whilst you're away. What is the working pattern that is going to be good for you in five, ten, or even fifteen years' time? As we all live longer, we'll be working longer, and if you love what you do, you're not going to want to give it up. And why?

As you work through this, keep moving backwards and forwards across the four W's to get richer descriptions for each ones. If working in luxury hotels is one of your 'wheres', then what does that mean for your who, what, and when? You will be creating an exciting personal and unique picture of your future.

And finally, to help you make this a little more concrete and take you into the action planning, ask yourself simply, 'What do I need to stop, start, or continue doing to achieve each of these?'

By the way, if you want to use a separate template for different horizons, go ahead and do so. Creating different futures can really help to crystalize and clarify your thoughts.

And here's the great thing: once you've decided on a new horizon, you can just go back to the beginning of the book and begin a whole new journey.

MINDSET

'We are what our thoughts have made us; so take care about what you think. Words are secondary. Thoughts live; they travel far.'

– Swami Vivekananda

Limitless

This part of the book could be considered an appendix, but to label it such would be to suggest it's not as important as the rest. In reality, it is probably the most important.

It is all about your mindset and how—and what—you tell yourself every day about what is possible is what will define your success. Your potential is truly limitless; you just have to remember that.

Running your own business is fulfilling, exhilarating, personally transforming, and fun. It is also, at times, lonely, difficult, frustrating, and tiring.

How we all respond to the down times is the difference between feeling half-full and feeling half-empty; it's responding not by caving in when things go wrong, but instead picking ourselves up, dusting ourselves down, and moving on; it's the difference between success and failure, and it's about choice.

We can choose how we respond. Sure, sometimes the pity party is a pretty attractive place to go, but turn that invitation down. There are far better and enriching ways for you to spend your time.

In this chapter I want to share with you some of my favourite exercises to keep you in that place of limitlessness. They are all designed to help move you from a place of feeling stuck into a place of freedom. (If you haven't spotted it yet, the seven sections of this book spell FREEDOM.)

Enjoy your business, and you will enjoy your life. The one obstacle you don't need in your way is you!

Confirming your value

This is an exercise to remind yourself that you do amazing work, create fantastic transformations, and add huge value to the clients with whom you work.

It will also provide you with fabulous copywriting material!

As with all these exercises, investing a small amount of time will reap huge rewards, so grab a cup of coffee, a pen and paper, and take fifteen minutes to do the following:

List forty ways that you bring value to your clients.

I know that you'll be able to write down the first six to ten pretty easily, but after that you'll no doubt start scratching your head. Keep on with it though because there is gold to be discovered here.

When you get stuck, look at it through some different perspectives.

- What will they take away?
- How will they feel?
- What will they understand?
- What will they be more capable of doing?
- How does what you do together impact on their life?

The list will easily expand, and suddenly, there in front of you is a long list of all the benefits that someone gets from working with you. Feel good?

So what can you do with this list?

- Have it near you to look at when you feel stuck or down or when things go a little awry.
- Pull out the three to five key priority results you create for your clients and use them to make your next web page, proposal, or piece of marketing material ping!
- And if you're feeling really brave, take one of the priority results and dig a little deeper into it.

This is the neatest and most useful exercise you can do to build your confidence, give you great marketing language, and create real clarity in your own mind about the value you bring. It also makes you feel good— something never to be sniffed at!

Positive imprinting

There are proactive ways to calm negative chatter in your head, and there are some more subtle ways that can help you create positive thoughts, running in the background, providing reminders of what it is you want and how you want to be so that you feel fulfilled and happy.

Imprinting is one way to do this.

What do I mean by imprinting? Imprinting is all about creating new patterns of thinking and shifting habits that are not serving you by surrounding yourself with new 'messages' to create new thinking and habits that will serve you well.

The old patterns and habits have come about from years of listening to others, whether that's teachers, friends, or family. They have formed through your personal experiences, they have been reinforced by what is around you, and, to be honest, they can be pretty firmly held. They are unhelpful and need to be replaced with something new.

So here are some ways to check in on how you might be unhelpfully imprinting your mind, and then we'll look at creating new imprints.

Let me start with a personal example of negative imprinting.

I want to lose some weight. Do I continue to watch the endless stream of cookery programmes on TV and buy magazines filled with recipes and gorgeous pictures of food I really shouldn't be eating, or do I shift my TV viewing (or stop viewing it altogether) and start reading healthy lifestyle magazines? And don't forget—those magazines are lying around my house, which means the imprinting continues because I keep seeing them.

Do I buy myself some new running gear so that I feel good when I'm out in the fresh air? More importantly, do I make sure I keep it all in a place where I can see it so that it reminds me I could be out exercising?

Do I move the contents of my fridge around so that I can see the healthy options as soon as the door is open (someone please get fridge manufacturers to move the salad drawer up!) instead of digging around at the back or the bottom?

Do I ensure that the first thing I do when it comes to sorting the diary for the week is to schedule exercise so that when I open the diary up each time—it's there?

This is all about creating constant, visual reminders of what you want to achieve or where you want to be.

You may just want to feel calmer. In that case, think about your environment. Does your house feel calm? Is your desk a calm space to be? Does your tablet or PC background have a picture that reminds you that calm is good for you?

If you're not feeling confident, what can you surround yourself with to remind yourself how good you are? Are there certificates that could be up on the wall that recognise your achievements? Are there pictures of you celebrating success that could be on show? With whom do you spend time—people who make you feel good, or people who suck the life out of you?

If you have noticed yourself dwelling on what is going wrong, create a space somewhere to put at least one Post-it up a day noting what has gone right. I promise you, you will have a great visual reminder that things are actually going pretty well, and you'll soon get really fed up of writing Post-its!

By doing all of these things, you will change the world you see around you. You will be choosing what you want imprinted on your mind, and it will bring you what it is you seek.

Stepping into your future you

I love this exercise. It's fun, it's a perspective shifter, and it creates instant impact. You'll love it.

I remember years ago when I was working in an organisation, one of the employees came up to me, disappointed that they had missed promotion—again. They looked so crestfallen and asked me for advice.

My question to them was what would they be doing differently if they were already working at that new level? How would they be behaving differently? They laughed! And then they started reeling off a list of how they would be.

I want you to do the same. Step into your future you.

Take just a few minutes and stop … breathe, open your mind, and think about where you want to be or what it is you really want. Is it about who you want to be? Is it about how you want your business to look? Is it about how much you earn or how much time you work—or don't?

Just spend a few minutes thinking yourself into that future space. Don't worry about how you will get there. Just put yourself out there in the future. How does it feel? Good, I'm sure.

Now that you are there, in that place, actually living the lifestyle you dream of, having the money you want, or working with really great clients—whatever that future is for you—from that space answer this question:

How will you deal with your week ahead?

Note down the actions you will take, how you will feel, and get into that place of energy and excitement.

Whenever you are in need of energy or feeling overwhelmed, take that step into your future you. Be powerful and feel the magic!

Achieving more – by doing differently

If you're looking for more time … there isn't any more.

You really need to choose wisely how you spend the time you have.

I know it's not easy to hear. I've spent my life 'squeezing in' as much as I possibly can. I used to constantly work out how I could do things smarter, more efficiently, faster—whether it was work, shopping, sorting out holidays, whatever. It was completely mad; I was doing all of this so that I had time—to do more!

So the mindset you need to embrace here is that to achieve more, you need to do less. This is what will make the seemingly impossible, possible.

It's about shifting your mindset significantly from a 'doing more' perspective to a 'doing differently' perspective. It's also about being confident enough to say no.

After all, there is no more time—just twenty-four hours in each day. And though sometimes the days might feel shorter or longer, they are, in fact, identical.

Once you accept and embrace that time is finite, you learn to negotiate with yourself within its boundaries and life becomes easier. Here are some things you could do:

- Move items from your to-do list into your diary—schedule them. This really helps you think about how long each task will take, which means fewer overrunning deadlines and less working late.

- Accept that doing something new or doing something different will be time-consuming (or might just feel it). Cooking your favourite dish might seem to take only minutes because you know exactly the steps you need to take and do half of them without thinking. Cooking a brand-new recipe can feel like it takes forever. New always feels a little clunky, so create time and space to cope with that clunkiness.

- Learn to say no to what isn't important. And if you are constantly saying yes and it's making you stressed, ask yourself why you are saying yes. The answer may reveal an opportunity to do things differently.

- Keep space for things to happen! There is magic in serendipity. If your diary is jam-packed every day of the week, there is no space for random good things to happen. Always schedule some unscheduled time!

- Switch off any alerts or notifications of e-mail, social media, or whatever. They will distract you from what you are doing and break your concentration.

- Schedule admin time (dealing with the above e-mails, alerts, etc.) once or twice a day, and spend the rest of the day focused on the client-getting tasks!

- Book holiday time out in your diary, and keep that time sacred. Recharging your batteries on a regular basis is essential.

Life is for living. Your business is part of life, not the whole of life.

You really can design the life you want. So when you're feeling overwhelmed, when work is piling up, ask yourself, 'What could I do differently?'

Sleep!

I've touched on recharging your batteries already by talking about taking breaks. The other really obvious way to recharge is to sleep really well when you go to bed.

Sometime back when I was pretty unwell, I went to see a specialist. He asked me if I felt refreshed when I woke in the morning. The question completely threw me. I had no idea what he meant. From that moment on, I began to appreciate the value of sleep and the difference it makes to life. When you run your own business, you must look after yourself—you are the business! So my final tip is how to sleep, really well.

There is lots of great advice out there on how to do so, from switching off all the gadgets to eating early. But there's one exercise I want to share with you that is blissfully simple and works perfectly every time.

Be grateful.

As you switch off the light and settle down for the night, think about all the things for which you are grateful from that day. It might be a new client. It might be finishing a piece of work. It might be that the sun came out, and you spent five minutes sitting and enjoying it. It might be the unexpected joke with a stranger or a call from an old friend.

Whatever happened that day, feel the gratitude flow through you.

Enjoy your business, enjoy your life, and sleep well.

About the Author and Her Business

Jo Dale is an award-winning leadership development consultant and coach with over 25 years' experience of helping individuals and organisations create success.

As well as working with a whole range of national and international organisations, in a variety of different sectors including investment banking, financial services, central government, further education and advertising, she also works with coaches and consultants to transform their expertise into powerful and profitable client-getting businesses that are high value, high integrity and done with elegance and ease.

Over the last 10 years Jo has run her own coaching and consultancy business with a focus on behavioural leadership and is appreciated by clients for her dynamic, pragmatic and highly perceptive style. She is seen as someone who is both practical and inspirational and is a quick and creative thinker with a sense of humour to go with it.

Jo strongly believes that we can all enjoy being leaders of our own lives and businesses and in doing so we enrich our own experiences and those of others around us.

She holds a BA in Modern Languages and an MSc in Organisational Behaviour from Birkbeck College (London University). She is Certified Practicing Co-Active Coach and is qualified by the British Psychological Society in a number of psychometric instruments.

Jo lives in Dorset with her partner and when not working, wonders whether she will ever complete the renovation of her 17th century house.

In Gratitude…

Thank you for your generosity in purchasing Get Clients 101 - The Essential Handbook for Coaches and Consultants.

I would be so grateful if you could take a minute or two to share what you loved about this book and provide an honest review on our Amazon sales page at http://bit.ly/ReviewGetClients101.

www.ingramcontent.com/pod-product-compliance
Lightning Source LLC
Chambersburg PA
CBHW060033210326
41520CB00009B/1112